A PEAK IN DARIEN

A Peak in Darien

FREYA STARK

JOHN MURRAY

Printed in Great Britain by
Cox & Wyman Ltd,
London, Fakenham and Reading
0 7195 3291 4

Dedicated
to my true and many
friends

Other Works by Freya Stark

Contents

Contents

Wood engravings by Reynolds Stone

Foreword

'Tis a bold venture, but not more bold than Columbus and many others, many of whom have arrived.

F. S. Letter 6.3.73

A FOREIGN FRIEND once told me that she had always loved England because of the colour that tinted it on maps (a colour that was of course spread pretty widely at that time).

Without any national prejudices about them that I can remember, I shared the liking for the coloured pages, and during a first long stay in hospital at the age of thirteen would ask for an atlas rather than a book and spend hours, and I think days, in following the mountain ranges and slanting rivers across any political shade they happened to express.

This passion for the surface of the world was satisfied for a number of years by mountain climbing. It taught me one of the basic rules of travel – to carry all one needs and nothing more – and gave that taste for Space in its own right which can destroy a nomad in captivity and could, I believe, kill many other people too if there were no means to create the open world inside one.

When the years of travel came, they justified everything that the coloured maps, and especially their emptier patches, had promised; and, now that I find actual journeys not so easy, they still feed me with their Ariel voices and make my world feel wider than it is. They belong to the past, but they have a kind of light that seems to me enduring and helps to prepare for what is still to come; and as those early journeys always took about two years of preparation, I decided – when I reached my eighty-first birthday – that the last one too should start with a certain amount of meditation before it and as much philosophy about an unmapped country as one's own uneducated power is able to absorb.

Hence these miniature essays. They are an explorer's gathering of what portable luggage one can legitimately take from Age's point of departure, which literature in general seems to have left rather pointedly alone. Plato gives old age a melancholy attention, pleased chiefly with the things it can no longer do; as I cast a cursory look for contemporaries down the succeeding centuries, it seems to me that those who wrote were in their fifties mostly, a signpost thirty years earlier than mine.

Caution, inspired perhaps by lifelong dealing with maps, has made my luggage extremely compact: it consists almost solely of an assumption, which I think most people would accept, that Space and Time are non-existent beyond our physical boundary. When these are eliminated with all their consequences, a great change appears in the unmapped white spaces which are the charm of every journey; airs of intangible freedom blow far beyond our range; and the words we have to use become constantly unsuited to the absence of our familiar barriers. The difficulty of language becomes very great.

Yet it is our own country in a sense more intimate than any we have ever travelled, for we ourselves are woven with its fibres, and words are left us here and there by travellers, as signposts on our way: but because of their elusive variety of language, and because of the conciseness of this booklet, I have made little recourse to them and have clung rigidly to my exclusion of Space and Time and to what that exclusion allows me to assume; in so doing I have given what is I believe a true and still enjoyable picture of the view that age can contemplate, spread out so inescapably before it.

Note: The essays in Part I should be read in sequence.

Part I
THE TIMELESS WORLD

Driving in twilight to Porto Raffi under the wave of Hymettos – a complicated feeling of home and safety in the darkening embrace of the land. Do animals know this, settling for the night? Was not tied to any place but generally to the shelter of the earth as such, and felt as if it were a very old sensation before our emergence as Man. The ending of summer and drawing on of winter and night seemed friendly, as if the earth were our natural nurse and protection and home.

F. S. from a diary 21.9.60

The Narrow Stream

What wise man will believe that the wind obeys the
dust?

FIRDAUSI. *Minuchihr*, Mole trans.

COUNTRY-BRED CHILDREN in England remember the
little streams that tumble from their moors. The places
for jumping them are well-known and there is no need to
go round by the bridges; and though a smooth run-up – for
which the valleys are often too entangled – would be
better, one can usually manage a few free paces for the
leap, and find a sloping boulder on the farther side. It
does not take long to learn that it is the arrival side that matters and its character must be gauged for an easy landing;
and the same may be said of old age in its last adventure
across its own inevitable stream. From whatever tangle of
thorns and brushwood we may reach it, that leap over-
arches the whole of Time and Space. Because we hope for
it as a beginning and not an end, it comes to be the only
thing that truly matters, and while our clock ticks on we
think about it, decently anxious that our landing may be
clean.

I lay drowsily in bed one morning, laid up for some
time with sciatica, and thinking of the South Teign, small
where it leaves the moors. I jumped across it on to a steep
boulder smooth as silk, and was surprised for a moment to
feel no slipperiness underfoot, not realizing that I was out
of Space and could slip no longer.

I knew the path very well and walked along it, noticing
dew still wet on the grass in shady places, and listening to

the tiny, shiny waterfalls happy in their noises below their screen of trees. The low valley was wild but not untended, and might have belonged in its casual carefulness to some philosopher or hermit, its pathway trodden out for one who walked alone; and I thought, as I strolled along, how, in other ages or lands, a monastery or chapel might have been placed in so quiet a view. I saw it there, with crowded saints and storied windows depicted by painters, architects and poets, 'in solemn troops and sweet societies' – immortality conceived from its first rude drawings in transitory mortal fashions of its day. A very few religions – the Byzantine for a short while – forbade human representation, and so did the Muslim for this world but made it up picturesquely for the next.

It was in the kindness of their intentions and in the desire to make a difficult subject as understandable as possible, that teachers and priests took, and take, the easiest road into the human heart. Uncounted millions must have been helped by the sight of eternal happiness or woe in their own image: but it has made things difficult for these of us who, believing in divinity in man, still like to put things in their places and cannot have them where they do not belong. The luggage we take across that narrow stream is not of our own choice; and it is fairly safe in an unsafe world to assume that Time and Space are no longer with us there.* This essay accepts that assumption, and tries to formulate what this separation entails.

It means, and this must be faced squarely, that the mortal image is lost from sight by eyes that are mortal, and with it are lost the human ways whose mixed ingredients and inexhaustible surprises contrived the human charm. This may have changed or been lost even within the legitimate borders of Time, and it is only the finality that appals us at its end; and is indeed the great divide of death. No consolation lies in denial, nor, when the loss is

* See Foreword.

deepest, can any comfort be found amid the sudden bleakness of our world. For ourselves, and for all we care for, our hope now lies across the river; and we are wise, as our strength fails and the days shorten, to live already a little beyond that border and walk in meditation along the farther bank.

There, in the consolation that awaits us, the barriers are down when Space and Time who erected them are safely pinioned to their terrestrial realm: and the power that is in us can flow without obstacle between past and present, or man and man, or God. And even in this earthly life there are moments of love or beauty that have surpassed their usual limitations and are ecstatic – rapturous – free that is of all apparent attachment, in a communion so close that the human agencies are lost to our consciousness and only the union remains. This is the citadel of that true God whatever we may call him, who moves in us undisturbed and in those we have loved; and also in those whom we may have been too late to know but have loved in our world through their labours: so that, relinquishing all but that divinity in us which crosses the river, we are un-fettered not in one portion or another, but in all.

This is that happiness which mystics have seen from the beginning of thought, from when some Greek discovered the word *infinity*: that comes here and there to our shackled side in a lifetime, so that ever afterwards its gentle light lies on our ways, and death opens like a flower even in rocky places, on its worldly stem.

This is what St. Augustine saw when he wrote of Freedom:

'. . hushed the images of earth, and waters, and air, hushed also the poles of heaven, yea the very soul be hushed to herself, and by not thinking on self surmount self; hushed all dreams and imaginary revelations, every tongue and every sign, and whatever exists only in transition . . . and He alone speak, not by them, but by Himself, that we may hear His Words, not through any tongue of flesh, nor Angel's voice, nor sound of thunder, nor in the dark riddle of a similitude, but might hear Whom in these things we love, might hear His Very Self without these; . . . could this be continued on, and other visions of far unlike be withdrawn, and this one ravish and absorb, and wrap up its beholder amid these inward joys, so that life might be for ever like that one moment of understanding which now we sighed after: were not this to "Enter into thy Master's joy"?"*

But before we reach it the river must be crossed, and one cannot be sure that some may not be found, even on that far side, to long for and think with nostalgia of the less perfect conditions of the lower bank: for the beauty of this world is largely due to its imperfections: and if there are visits and revisits to this planet from those not yet quite ready for peace, it may be that purgatory is their own inclination and not punishment at all. All is on the road, and the incidents are not to cause discouragement if the terminus is safe.

The dew was now dry by the side of the path along my valley, and I found, of course, no great difficulty in slipping back to the lower side.

* *Confessions of St. Augustine*: Book IX, par. 25.

2

A Link in the Chain

Nothing is so delicate and fugitive by its nature as a
beginning.
PIERRE TEILHARD DE CHARDIN. *The Phenomenon of Man.*

MY LODGING is in an old house on the city wall (for
Asolo was once a small defendable city on its hill).
A little terrace juts out where I can write and watch
cherry blossom clustered round every cottage, now
sinking in its first green leafage into the background of the
plain. The shallow valley with the curve of its two hills is
like a cradle which beauty fills and overflows to its horizon,
and I am happy to be inside it and swinging with it in its
tiny way with the swinging world. In the contented
laziness of spring the mist that hides the edges of the plain
is but thin gathered sunlight: the mind wanders to other
plains beyond it, hills and seas and cities, to the rim of a
world's life that is rounding like our own selves to its
peace. Eternity is all about us and awareness climbs
through the millennia or the centuries or the years,
through changes that are footholds for Time and must stop
when Time stops. And a wonder comes at what stage of
consciousness, what point of progress through terrestrial
aisles, the breakthrough of immortality occurred?

Though our 'permanent' geography is simplified by the
absence of Space and Time this terrestrial question is not
answered; and theology, which makes the transition from
mortality more gradual with expedients such as purgatory
or other pauses, is irrelevant, because these too are travelling in Time and Space.

Our concern is not with them, but with that further earthly frontier whence, neither up nor down nor forward, but altogether, the ageless spirit *is* in its simplicity of being: 'in sua volontade è nostra pace.'*

We wonder with hope and timidity if in our gradual world we can reach that freedom. In these moments of insight it is well, I think, to look back and see how far we have come, with the dark still unfinished before us.

The fluid rocks have settled, the seas beat against their cages; and life has crept along veins of moisture with no one to watch its birth. In rainfalls the forests have grown and flourished and decayed; the slow amphibians walked about them and were forgotten; the swamps fell desolate, and newer animals in their variety moved and mated and died. Man stood upright and sharpened his tools and began his story, that continues to be woven like a garland in its orbit round the sun. At some point from that swaying rootless insecurity he met his Revelation and became conscious of the indestructible presence of God. Whatever this may have been called, it appeared and was believed, and was the greatest moment of an earthly world which is our ornament and bondage. Divinity appeared dim and intermittently visible on our planet, undatable except that some consciousness must have been ready to receive it without record in the distance of its youth, at some time between the rain swamps and the first philosophers.

When I see my dog occasionally looking with a desperate and pathetic longing to know what I am saying, I would like to take him with me into the abstract ring: but one cannot say more than that at some moment before history some creature asked a question and obtained an answer. Time had become securely linked to what was endless and timeless in the monologue on earth which had turned to conversation.

Before the question was asked and the answer given,

* Dante: *Paradiso III*, Piccarda Donati.

earth travelled unenlightened and unaware, built by clouds and rocks, and winds and sunlight, and animals and trees. Unconscious of sorrow, they cradled the jewel of Eternity in their firmament, and advanced it through their own universe lit by their own stars; and every step was chiselled by these unconscious unrewarded artisans, each period bearing the weight of the whole chain as they lifted it from past to future, for the weakest link must yet be able to bear the weight of the whole or the chain breaks. Thus they did their work here, unaware of Time and yet before timelessness on earth was known.

For a long period the question must have hovered, seeking its entry through dimness of minds where the abstract was strange. One can see it in dogs and dolphins, and quite lately I came upon a large photograph of two chimpanzees in a Swiss clinic where they looked out, mother and daughter I guessed, closely embraced in what looked to me – but was probably not to them – unuttering sadness, as if the brain were a letter-box for letters never to be sent. Their fingernails were eaten away like those of poor peasant women through small and oft-repeated labours, and many lines between their eyebrows were creased in a perpetual passive expression of strain: keepers of our inheritance, they had lifted their world and ours towards its moment, and sat at its shut door giving no sign except the possibly misleading but surely puzzled load of those puckered brows.

But we pass freely, and if it were not for the witness of mystics and saints and poor pilgrims who have seen it, would scarcely notice that there is a door at all. And as I look out over my valley I am happy in the loves that have slowly trained it like a climbing blossom to meet the timeless immortality of man.

3

Unfair

> For it is the height of unreasonableness to be guilty
> of impiety towards the gods because one is angry
> with men.
>
> POLYBIUS, XI,7.

FAIR AND UNFAIR are among the most influential words in English and must be delicately used. "It is not that I mind being robbed," one of my godsons (legitimately) complained; "but it is so unfair." But the wretch picking his pocket probably thought about unfairness too, and the heart of the matter was some obliterated starting point when equity's balance was lost. If we track one injustice after another across the wastes of ages, we will come in time to two desert altars where Cain and Abel, and Jehovah himself, looked at the same act from opposite directions.

Neither Nature nor any Divinity invented or discovered by man ever presented fairness as an essential in a world imprisoned in Space and Time. Free of these shackles, ubiquitous and yet our own substance, there is, we believe, an incorporeal home close to and indeed within us, which many have known. But in spite of Revelation we have learnt little enough about it, and it seems to me that there is a certain impertinence in assuming our own rules to be binding both here and there. Since fairness is discouraged by Nature and not attended to by God, we also may assume that on the far side of Time and Space it is not needed.

Having got so far in my meditation, I reopened the

subject and pointed out to my godson that, if interested, he could always enlarge his point of view by looking at it from the other side, where the inevitability of being cheated if rich would appear as a mere link in the long chain of causes and effects, and could be accepted with philosophy. I then began to consider (to myself) what a fair and unfair world would look like side by side if they existed; and found, to my surprise, the fair one dull.

There was in it a want of our mixed world's surprises, and its good too near an investment or to those household accounts (not mine however) that tally at the end of their month or century or year. In our world where nothing tallies and fairness is unsuccessful, it is yet an actual meeting place half way between your house and mine. It does not seriously diminish the gamble of life, but can encourage when generosity stumbles, or, heroically, support weakness when the warmer love for humanity flags. By its mere direction towards the rights of others it develops an unselfish liberality, and – in its nobler reaches – a readiness to pay the difference oneself.

The list of 'fairness' virtues makes it obvious that our temporal world would be extremely handicapped without them: and my godson's exclamation was the cry for a raft that might at any moment save us all from drowning. It is our need that makes us follow our own saints rather than God or Nature, and try to express the outlines of their love with our inferior colours; and so we practise fairness on earth as best we can.

But what if it succeeds? (There is no fear of it, for the timeless rudder is steady). If that *could* be, we should lose our most happy surprises – and unhappy ones too, that break a path for charities unknown. We should lose many of the uncertainties of life, that at this moment are pressing rather heavily upon us, but yet give us our chances – to forgive and be forgiven, to sin and to repent, and to rejoice in people whose failings may be other than our own.

Unfair

In the bloodshed of the Renaissance, appalling even by our standards, St. Catherine of Siena converted a young nobleman who was soon after captured by the rival party and condemned to the scaffold. As a last gift from his saint he begged her to stay beside him in his last moment; and so she did, and knelt, and smoothed his neck on the block so that the axe might cut clean; and took the head from her lap where it fell, and buried it. Words are not made to express this depth or gauge the depth in which it is received. But the world in which it can happen even once is a good world in spite of all.

When we reach the edge where our bones doff their garments, and our weakness and our strength are both to be discarded, we may understand how Evil helped us in our day.

On that last barrier, *flammantia moenia mundi*, in that unimaginable transparence, as our boats put into the Unity of which we are a part, we may imagine those comrades – Courage and Prudence, Temperance, Truthfulness, Justice and many others, and Fairness among them, looking out beyond their own climate on an adventure that needs them no longer; and see them turn back – arm in arm perhaps? – with the opposites they must go on fighting while Time and Space endure.

4

The Conscious Personality

Love, the awakened heart, travelling towards its treasure.

PATRICIA NAPIER

IN THE AEGEAN SPRING, if one sails in some Greek cockle shell from island to island, one may cross the sea of Samos where it is seventy fathoms deep. When the winds are quiet, a sapphire smoothness extends too dark to be transparent; and upon it the wake from our keel builds spangles and triangles and a myriad fancies of foam. So brilliant is the contrast that it seems impossible for depth to produce this effervescence, which presently sinks and submerges and is dissolved in the darkness that made it: and I have sometimes fancied that if those glittering particles were infused with conscious purpose added to their variety, a likeness might be imagined with the human race emerging in separate and individual awareness until it too is once more absorbed.

We have been following Time and Space and have assumed that there is no temporal quality beyond their frontiers; and human conscious *personality*, while its heavenly flashes are laden with earth, can be allowed no probability of survival except in an atmosphere where Time and Space exist. A third medium must be assumed, not of restraint but of liberation, to free the divinity in man, and many mystics have recognized this as a strength of love and joy impelling all things – sun and stars as Dante saw them, or the rapturous invocation of St. Paul. I too, not as a theologian but as a traveller, adopt the assumption and believe it to be true, recognizing Love and Joy as timeless embodiments of the divine. Alone among the virtues of earth we take them to move freely beyond its temporal borders, where it is my belief that all cruelty, all corruption, all wickedness are shed, and Time and its virtues and vices, and the beauties of earth and the sins of men, drop away under the greater wings of peace.

Even in imagination one cannot step into this eternity without meeting the most human problem of *personality*, the individual survival when Space and Time have vanished and Love alone lives on because it is a part of divinity itself. Eternity we carry in us and have watched its manifestation, unrecorded but undoubted, in the unconscious world among the first questionings of man. Where the door shut on my poor chimpanzees (essay 2) we entered into the divine immortality: and our survival depends on what shred of this marvel we can carry beyond the grasp of Time. The words of our prayer, 'on earth as it is in heaven', are the recognition of a fundamental visitation, the sharing in a unity which is itself and ever has been, disclosed and mingled in our universe with its terrestrial spheres.

This gift, more widely scattered than we imagine, may reach into very sombre darknesses of human earth: 'Even a beetle is beautiful in the eyes of its mother' the Arab proverb tells us: and I have kept through many years the letters of one whose son was executed justly enough according to our laws and in the flux of time will be forgotten, but who lived in her memory in the gentleness of his childhood and of her heart.

The valiance of Love is tested under scorching rays; even beneath consciousness we know it to be victorious, and its small household details or kindness among strangers carry a radiance that can turn the help of human beings even into one of the comforts of war. As the abstract, to most of us, is insufficient, we gather – unless we are saints –

what human comfort we can from any stray light of everyday that may cling where the Everlasting spills over into our waste of Time. The virtues we are accustomed to, and the cruelties we are inured to, go from us, but its trifles survive when their substance and that of eternity are the same.

Years ago I fell asleep in a train in England and woke to see a cup of tea on the table before me. "You looked so tired," said the unknown woman opposite: "I brought it for you as I was getting mine."

When I was young, the old friend in whose house we lived would play Beethoven or Bach in the sitting-room below to give me pleasure while I dressed in the morning. The summer garden breathed in at the windows mixed with the familiar sounds, and all is clearly graven in my mind: and though it must fade, with sight and hearing and human heart – yet I still feel in that gentle atmosphere an element to which we all belong, a link whose expression and recognition must rely on some medium here unknown.

Separateness can perhaps exist with unity, as fingers in a hand that still keep their own feelings in their subordinate way. And what we must ever remember is that our world is young. Its Time cannot last like the eternity of Love,* but its orbit is not yet completed, its steps round the sun have aeons of life before them, and may change, or step into the nothingness of its own destruction, or gain new revelations in their course. We believe that in flashes of insight eternity has spoken, and have no certainty that all was heard or very much is known. But the freedom of choice lies with us, and we believe Love to be eternal, and we know that Time and Space must end.

---

* The transformation of Love is the miracle celebrated by the Eucharist in the Christian faith. It welds the humblest timebound food of earth into a presence of divinity, exaltation and submission. I am no theologian but I believe this mystery; I have not taken its evidence only because it penetrates beyond the strictly geographic nature of what I am using.

5

Joy

The difference lies in the listener's heart.
If he would forget he lives at the world's end
The bird would sing as it sang in the palace of old.
     PO CHU-I: 'Hearing the Oriole.' A.D. 818,
     Arthur Waley trans.

JOY IS A QUEEN of virtues, apt to be neglected by theologians, or anyway relegated to a world other than ours. Christianity, apart from some mystics and the earliest Greek Fathers, often forgets her earthly divinity, though her opposite (despondency or accidia) is numbered among the seven deadly sins. Basic as love, Joy does, I believe, keep its virtue both inside and outside of Time; and when we have shed all else that helped our earthly life Love and Joy remain, and must have warmed a roughly sketched universe long before immortality disclosed itself on our planet. The sea-anemones in their dim gardens, where the rhythm of waves drops and lifts their acquiescent petals, perhaps already registered the unconscious arrival of joy.

When *possessions* came and, being girt with limitation, grew by their nature into prisons, they were able to give pleasure rather than joy, and the true art of living came to be largely centred on keeping them in their proper place – sustaining but subordinate. The people I have most loved and admired were never distracted by them: enjoyments could be bought but Joy was independent, and the thought of it brings back to me the picture of an old and happy man, Admiral Sir William Goodenough, who was President of the Royal Geographical Society and gave me the first award I ever got – the Back grant of £40 (which seemed a large sum then) for my first Persian journey.

The Royal Geographical Society's beautiful house looked upon its task in the light of helping those eager to help themselves, and Sir William, 'The Old Admiral', believing in this excellent principle, took every promising new traveller to his heart. I think with affection of all the years that followed, when one would find him in the little office where he sat, and talk about any adventure in one's mind at the moment. Much loved, he and his wife, both blue-eyed and white-haired, would sit every Sunday at either end of their long luncheon table in the country, and entertain people who had done this or that in most corners of the world.

"He has just come from the Shan States" – would introduce some shy and promising young man: "Oh, you turn from Burma to the right" – if more detail was asked for.

I saw him last on a summer morning when the Second World War was still moaning above us with V.1's while he showed me the bits of his ship from the battle of Jutland, which he cherished. When very ill, some old shipmate said to him: "You must be unhappy, tied to your bed?"

"Oh no," said the Old Admiral. "I've got to be ill, but I won't be unhappy too."

I often think of him and of the steadfastness of his tough generation, and how his happiness, planted so deep below vicissitude, could be thought of as the very substance of delight. He welcomed it as if it were roses on his path – to be welcomed and not clung to – (for the plucked rose must die).

> 'Oh, no man knows
> Through what wild centuries
> Roves back the rose.'*

* Walter de la Mare.

Joy

Blossom upon blossom through its ages, into a future with the hands of unknown gardeners upon it, even to the rose of men's imagination and the end of Time – when so looked at, Joy in its freedom embraces and enhances all happy ownerships and temporary pleasures inherent in whatever loveliness or riches the world can pour upon us: to lose sight of their evanescence pushes the possessive moment too far.

For Joy belongs to that Unity in which, without usually knowing it, we live. It meets itself suddenly in small things as in great, and recognizing itself sets off this delight. Its variety is endless – words hitherto dormant, or the recognition of human strangers one with another; or runs of music that wander through our hearts; or a wayside view, or the taste of seasons, or the mere sparkle of sunlight on a stream. Sometimes it is a gesture, and I can remember a long and weary waiting-room in the highlands of Turkey when a woman's hand set this off as she adjusted her baby in its shawl; the wind was howling outside and suddenly this hand, this magic, so beautiful and tender, shaped itself through the ages, embodying the thoughts and loves and wickedness of man; until, at a meeting of lives so different, this woman and I smiled at each other over the little Turk wrapped in his shawl between us.

Most things animate or inanimate can thus be a stimulus to joy if there is warmth in the heart to receive and answer their implicit unity. Some awareness is required to show that we recognize and love, or at any rate are pleasantly surprised by any small note in the great welter that surrounds us. If we do not respond, the spark falls dead for lack of feeling, and with such wasted joys the paths of life are strewn. A cherry tree grew against our wall in a London garden. We would wait for its blossom in spring and pause to look up as we walked beneath it, and on one occasion, returning from some absence, tired and with a headache, I stopped to gaze as usual, and the magic had gone. It was there, but I could not see it: the cherry was wasting its beauty and we could not *unite*. Husbands and wives and lovers come upon these moments and waste the spark which runs through all things, which only unity engenders from the beginning and probably before the beginning of Time: its gentle divinity, so inextricably mixed with all that our world has ever contained and much beyond it, is, with love, the chief ally we have in this world's war.

For whatever our God may be, He takes no ostensible side in our battles, apart from the strength He gives intrinsic to Himself: but Joy is our ally, and the bond of all union through the ages, and not to be parted from whatever sorrowful frontier we may have to cross.

6

Happiness on the Treviso Road

Yet neither loss of friends, nor an emptying future,
nor England nor the ruin of long-builded hopes,
so far have taught my obstinate heart a sedate
deportment.

From a newspaper – anonymous

THE ROAD from my house to Venice, only forty-two
miles away, was planted ever since I can remember
with plane trees, or perhaps sycamores, a rank on each
side. A traveller from Alpine valleys, or from Friuli in
the east, might think himself approaching the lagoons
through a long and winding avenue. Driving here in
winter the asphalt glitters crisp and frozen, and the fugitive stems, almost the same colour, sway curve beyond
curve: one might be following the backbone of a snake on
the great Venetian plain, peaceful and quiescent in its
coils. As I drove there one morning, the butterfly feeling
of happiness folded its wings for a moment and settled
on my heart. The sight of these trees always brought it –
young with young leaves like a mist in spring, heavy in
autumn like metal, grateful with summer shade or filtered
in winter sunlight that drew Japanese patterns on the
ground:

O wisdom and money
How can you requite
The honey of honey
That flies in that flight?
The useless delight?

35

What benefactors they are. Hundreds of people travel
here through every busy hour and to every one of them –
whether they recognize it or not – a little crack of happiness is shown.

I had got so far in my thoughts when a block ahead made
me slow down and I saw a bulldozer at work; in the ditch
beside the road lay the trunks of four great veterans
already felled.

"Why are they cutting the trees?" I asked a group of
labourers standing there with their picks.

"They hit the motorists," was the reply, redolent of the
world's injustice. I drove along saddened and shattered,
through clouds of dust made by the bulldozers, and began
to do some arithmetic in my head. Not more than about
one motorist is likely to be killed during the time that
thousands are driving along under the trees. How many
moments of beauty are required to make the life of a
rather careless motorist expendable? We are poor reason-
ers, but it seemed to me that the sum of general happiness
was greater when the trees in their splendour could hit a
motorist now and then.

No one goes to battle thinking he may be killed: it is an
old saying among soldiers, and far less will the fear of
death prevent people from enjoying themselves – or why
should they smoke cigarettes? or live on the slopes of
volcanoes? or go to sea like the fishermen of Barbadoes
with not a notion how to swim? If they recognize happiness they will achieve it at the risk of their life. At this
moment a more than usually absent-minded swerve of my
front wheels brought me rather sharply up against the
problem, and I waited for a leisurely stroll in my garden to
think it out further.

Happiness, I mused, looking out over the Venetian
plain – sunlit houses and increasing incrustation of
factories along every one of its straight smooth roads.
Every farm has a frigidaire, and a television set in hope

if not in fact: and prosperity has brought contentment, whirling round corners on motor-cycles, or packing itself for Sundays into the family car. Forty years ago we used to meet these people clip-clopping on wooden sabots by quiet dusty roadsides where the girls could stroll with their knitting and graze their sheep in the ditches. It would be grudging indeed not to feel pleasure in the sight of so much new comfort in the sun.

C'est magnifique, mais ce n'est pas la guerre. Contentment is not the same as happiness, and words should stick to their meaning. This that they call by her name is indeed contentment, *contained* in enclosure, such as the young Russians in Uzbekistan may feel, whose food and wages are guaranteed at last; they too are content – and why not? A miracle of two generations has lifted them from lives of continual poverty and privation, and within their barricades they can feel at peace.

But happiness, no philanthropist, goes on a separate way, follows her own laws, and feeds on her own moments. They are short and deep; and these two adjectives are essential for a substance so fine which deals in the immortal.

"I have never been more happy," my godfather said to me, as we watched his last dawn throw roses on the Alps before he died.

Fragility and death have no part in this goddess, but they are shadows cast by a sun that shines upon her; and they are never far when she is near:

> The folk who are buying and selling;
> The clouds on their journey above;
> The cold wet winds ever blowing;
> And the shadowy hazel grove
> Where mouse-grey waters are flowing
> Threaten the head that I love.
>
> W. B. YEATS

So beauty appears threading her trackless way. A menace is enclosed even in her most trifling apparition; it may be no more than the end of temporal things, and the inevitable cooling of our planet. But I have no wish at this moment to venture on love or death or friendship or even the artist's vision, a happiness profound as any. I am thinking of light, pleasant, delicate surprises, that meet us all the time.

The sound of the wind, for instance. To everyone their happinesses come in a separate manner, and to me – who am naturally inclined towards the abstract – the world's enchantment rustles in the skirts of the wind. I think of it dancing in sunlight on thin sands, or straining at the oak boughs in Dartmoor valleys, and the strong walls of my house feel safe and yet free, cradled in that moaning crooning song.

A sort of ecstasy of surprise and joy came to me with the first reading of the (translation) text of the Iliad during a bad Atlantic crossing – a feeling so strong that I had to leap out of my bunk and sway up and down the cabin with the swaying ship.

There must always be a touch of ecstasy in true happiness, because of her divine origin; she slips in with a release from all constriction, the lark's song in Dante's paradise. I speak for myself alone, for as I say there is much variety, but to me she often comes as something external which may be, and perhaps usually is, not closely related to myself.

Millions of such moments remain, remembered or forgotten, gay as a passing glance or loaded with some gleam of their intrinsic depth – for the genuine character of happiness is never shallow; her slightest moment grows, like any plant or flower, from the whole substance of earth. No government or municipal decision can therefore create her, since they lack the ingredients of which she is made: the most they can do is to build her a livable climate, and this they try to do, in many dedicated ways; the trouble remains that they are not often aware of what happiness is.

She is not, for instance, economic. She will be found in places as bare as those muscle diagrams which show the human body without its skin. With warmth either too little or too much and just enough food to live on, I have often been surprised in a hut or round a camp fire by the carefree faces that surround one: poverty neither helps nor hinders – unless it is too extreme – and riches often take away the world's up and down variety which is one of the things that keep us awake to the unknown.

The Unknown, the inseparable, the X in our pattern of life; if I had to give a one-sentence-definition of happiness, I should call it the conscious or unconscious awareness of this Unknown. It has cradled the human race out of its earliest shadows, and as our circuits widen, the shadows simply grow: the vista of discovery, not the completed box, keeps the scientists happy; anything consummated palls, because the unknown has ceased to surround it; I can remember in my own life the boredom of my doll's house when all its furnishing was done.

Now the strangest thing is that governments nearly always are blind to this fundamental rule and try to provide happiness by clearing all its possibilities away. They are splendid with keep-off-the-grass municipal gardens – which give pleasure and not joy – but required the crisis of the First World War and no happiness in question to think of the allotment, where a man can watch his radishes break out of the unexplored soil. The English rapture, which in its sober way can survive most things, seems to me to be symbolized by her rows of small front gardens, each separate enthusiasm enjoying the individual surprises of the spring. Long may they flourish!

Administration will make us happy, the governments continue to think, in spite of evidence heaped in piles of debris round them – and would continue, for instance, to take from the poor Cypriots (if they were still being administered) the pleasure of racing each others' cars on their highway which might have kept their minds off politics now and then, for there is, after all, a touch of infinity in speed.

This touch of infinity the human being needs in every breath of his being – in literature, architecture, all art and personal relations. It is recognized not only in a Shakespeare tragedy that leaves us shaken but satisfied, drowned as it were in life, but in plays like *Waiting for Godot* whose squalor held the same quality of secret and trans-temporal awareness. It is only the immortality of its trifles that can keep the lightest comedy alive.

All this is recognized but partitioned off as it were from everyday life, of whose small continuous commerce with infinity most government appears to be unaware. Whole slabs of time are made impervious to joy by the fact that things have to be written out in triplicate, and the trees of the Treviso road are being cut down.

7

Solitude

The loveliest thing on earth a shadow had
A dark and livelong hint of death
Haunting it ever till its last faint breath . . .
Who then may tell
The beauty of Heaven's shadowless asphodel?
WALTER DE LA MARE: 'Shadow'

A SMALL BRONZE IDOL of mine found in Luristan has two faces that look in opposite directions from a miniature pillar; and I often wonder what sort of elasticity produced this fancy. What the ancient Lurs attributed it to I do not know – but I myself came to think of *Solitude* as the owner of these two opposite aspects so definitely emphasized, and I look at the bronze profiles sometimes with affection, and sometimes with fear.

Solitude has now survived to be perhaps my earliest friend. His thoughtful and kindly presence stands at the edge of every landscape I can remember. A vague companion, never clearly visible yet never wholly absent, unobtrusive but persistent, I would become suddenly aware of him sometimes in autumn when mists crept nearer to the paths, and the evenings were drawing in; or again as I rode early in the morning, cubbing over the moors when the first sunlight hung on spider-webs in the gorse.

I soon realized that with this comrade the animals whom a human voice would have disturbed continued to sprint about our horses' feet as if we were not there. And gradually in his company and through his silence I came to realize that solitude is not loneliness, but rather the mingled voice of all things attending to their separate affairs. As the years went by, I came to recognize how fortunate was my early introduction to one who is to be the last of our companions, whose later face can be both cruel and severe.

*   *   *

Homer tells us that the lives of men are like leaves on the mountain sides of Pthira that fall in autumn and are renewed in spring. The loneliness of their old age is an inevitable pattern, not too hard for them to bear while something still remains to attach their shrunken tendrils to the stem, though Life itself is falling right and left into the arms of darkness.

There is however a more intimate loneliness of quite a different sort: it is our own withdrawal, unrelated to our fellows, rooted in ourselves. It is intrinsic and inevitable, and takes from us comforts and amusements of life too strong for us to bear. The sympathy of friends, unable to help, can only, like a late sunlight, gild the unfathomed surface of this cold. It is the desert of Age which must be crossed to its unseen conclusion.

On this last traverse, Solitude gives his sternest profile and walks beside us more as a jailor than a friend. Happy we are who can remember his kinder aspect and, as we look from increasing bleakness, can still recognize the magic comrade in the map of years that lies so far behind.

A strange metamorphosis comes into the light of these static landscapes under their faded suns, and we suddenly see that the presence was not Solitude only, but the whole meaning of the world, of all worlds, their skies and storms and creatures, their voices and their silence. Solitude allowed these things to talk and cleared away the enlargement of our own selves in the view – this mask – our

42

sheath and prison – that communicates with others equally fallacious, whose fabricated contours crowd our life. Rarely recognized and rarely truthful, they have little to do with the essential stream, which Sorrow or love or rapture can pierce and make us conscious of, and which Solitude too is able to compel. In his presence we looked out and did not need to find Self in the foreground; and the people whom Solitude has befriended can be recognized by the undemanding candour of their ways.

I have reached the age when the desert is closing about me, and Solitude comes now and then to take me on my way. And, as I have known him so long, I can ask what makes him now so different and so grim.

"It is the desert," says he, "You must cross it and I must cross it with you – and I too am one of those who die where it ends, for there is no Solitude beyond the frontiers of Space. Our desert is full of phantoms – illusion among illusions, of which I am one. And people see me and are afraid. But at the skyline I leave you. No one beyond the boundary will want to contemplate himself."

"Solitude," I said sadly. "You are surely not telling me that I shall not see you there?"

"You may not see me: I shall be there; but with another name."

8

Heroism

'Madam, the wings of opportunity are fledged
with the feathers of death.'

FRANCIS DRAKE to Elizabeth

One can't feel sure of oneself. The X in life is
what one must feel sure of.

F. S. diary 1.9.67

I REMEMBER, years ago above Zermatt, a hotel whose
name I have lost. It stood in a hollow between Breithorn
and Lyskamm and Matterhorn himself.

Lying there in bed before the climb, listening to the
moving avalanches answering each other before the ice of
midnight froze their tumult, I lay in a panic fear. There
was no particular thought of catastrophe behind it, but
it made me feel as if I were adventuring beyond my powers
to challenge those resounding voices of the night. The time
came to switch on the light, to fasten the stiff cold boots of
those days and – half asleep though comforted with coffee –
to walk out under the stars. But it was not till the hut had
been reached and left, and indeed till my fingers had the
friendly wrinkles of the granite in their grasp, that Fear
vanished and a bond with the mountain in our coming
struggle, an intimacy – of tension and resistance, a strange
affinity with love – came and remains.

This sort of emotion young soldiers must take to battle,
with its natural mosaic of timidity and courage, and
confidence in their luck and their escape. A producer of
heroism, it is not in itself heroic; the presence of any
natural hero is enough to emphasize the stretch that lies

between. The unlikeliness of rescue marks the difference, and the beaches of Dunkirk had chances which a captain waiting to sink with his ship cannot hope for; nor could the final camp of Scott in the Antarctic; nor the Greek girls dancing off their precipice to escape the oncoming soldiers; nor the Lacedaemonians on their sea-wet rock. Death was the only way out for them, and the influence of their remembered deeds is very great; and so perhaps is that of those apparently unnoticed. Their quality will remain as long as man, or even animals, remain (for what devotion can surpass the heroic devotion of dog or horse?) But that which breathes in the human heroism, separating it from everyday courage, is the *expectation and acceptance of defeat*.

'All hours wound; the last one kills', the Romans said: and humanity accepts the necessity of death – indeed it has to do so – with at least an appearance of calm. The fears of youth are winds from outer spaces, they give a shiver and pass; their end also is defeat in this world. But it is the old that must usually negotiate the Inevitable. Like Monsieur Jourdain talking prose without knowing it, they can be heroes in their own despite.

This universal chance for heroism – the aristocrat among virtues – is laid in our general lap within reach of us all. However poor, however despised, however worn with the squalor of life, the old can find opportunity rather than doom in the Inflexible that presses so closely upon them. Its mask is not that of the hero we recognize: no nimbus surrounds it except, in most cases, the bodily suffering that is the toll it takes: its hope is for relief rather than triumph, if it hopes at all: and anyway you may say that the element of choice is missing.

This, however, is not true, for the hero's choice lies, as we have seen, in the *acceptance* as well as in the expectation of defeat. It lies in man's own will, and through their later years of hardship, discouragement or sorrow many

old people discover it; their eyes, like sailors' eyes, grow
vague and clear to hold their own horizons; their sight,
their hearing, their active strength, their memory too has
left them, and yet – without knowing it – they stand in the
gate when the inadequate garrison has scattered, and
capture, in that transcendent moment, not the praise of
men but their own intimate solace and repose.

We are not Christian in our general modern attitude to
death; whatever pain it may take us from, it is lamented
and if possible ignored and definitely avoided in conversation; and the Muslim mother can teach us something when
she answers: 'the glory be to God', to those who sorrow
with her for her children. Faith is a handrail, yet in this
matter of heroism I have found much steadiness in those
who die without it. In his facing of it the born hero acts
independently according to the springs of his own nature:
his belief in immortality is not necessary. The poetry of
Lucretius and most of the pagan literature take the sadder
side.

These essays are not written for believers, but for such
among us as are willing to advance as far as honest but
purely mundane evidence can take them, and the route is
geography rather than religion (though the terminus is
probably the same). The virtues that faith teaches are still
essential, whatever the form they take, but the Hero has
his own truth and not that of the world in general to
conduct him to his end. This takes him across the barriers
of self and into his freedom: his own nature carries him and
there is nothing he need fear.

But most of us are not likely to be more than fleetingly
heroic as we take our general chance at the gates of death.
The Self we have lived with has perhaps been an ornament
and a help through our world, has been called by many
names not usually ignoble and cherished by many virtues
of enterprise and courage until its bourn is reached. Here,
with or without religion, it must be slipped out of, and if

weakness or a time of suffering and sickness precede this moment, that too must be adjusted in the laborious choice.

The chance is given and the choice is ours; and Life, divesting us of all we need no longer, can wrap us in a sheath of splendour, if we wish it, at life's end. Free of Self, the world in its battlefield nakedness grows beautiful: the morning breezes play with harp-sweet fingers, the gossamer mists trail round their mountains, the small leaves in the sun dance to their own shadows, the humans walk to their works with Time before and after, and to us – actors no longer, with no possessive ghost to hold us – the climate of Eden returns.

I go back to the Matterhorn at dawn. We reached the top ridge that separates the Swiss and Italian slopes. Far, very far below but clear because of steepness, two valleys, one in either country, slid through their shadows, and Weisshorn – most beautiful of mountains – lifted its perfect triangle in the north. The ridge is sharp and cannot be more than a foot wide, for I was prepared to straddle my way into Italy for some twenty minutes along it; but the good guide said: 'We must walk free – free as if it were a street.' And so we did.

9

Landscape of Age

The westering Phoebus' horse
Paws in the ancient dust as when he shocked
The earth with rising.
    FRANCIS THOMPSON: 'Anthem of Earth'

WHEN YOUNG I used sometimes to stay in Edinburgh, beautiful and beloved city, with Professor and Mrs. MacCunn and their daughter who is my friend though we see each other rarely. The Professor's wife was a delicate writer and full of pleasant remarks, and as we stepped out one autumn morning, above the valley where mists were gleaming in sunlights of their own, "I often think of the celestial city," said Mrs MacCunn, "when I look into the valley through the mist."

Many landscapes begin to look like that as one grows old, their enchantments enhanced by life's incrustations – as trees for instance continue to carry with them an atmosphere of the innumerable times we met them, a shimmer remembered among their varied branches as elusively as if they were dancers in and out of their coloured veils. After its youthful surprises the beauties of landscape gradually reveal themselves as things of intimacy rather than strangeness, and one comes to conclude that the true fruit of travel is perhaps the feeling of being nearly everywhere at home: it has taken many years to realize that the sun of Himalaya and our own sun are intrinsically the same, and no diversity, however exceptional, can be more stimulating than this interesting familiarity. A view that we meet many times, or that has a similarity in various places, acquires a richer profusion and a wider meaning: the single voice so poignant in our youth comes to be reinforced and to thrill with the breadth and depth of an orchestra, and old age can weave the magic of life itself into a complicated picture – the future close before, the past with all its implications far behind, and life's fragility visible along that slender bridge.

The *movement* of landscape holds us when increasing deafness or failing sight require an intercourse more penetrating than that of words, and the regimented shadows sweeping over mountain ranges, the clouds above them whose wayward strategy depends on the great currents of the air – they come to speak with voices of their own. Birds in their lower strata will congregate about the eaves of some outstanding tower – in the high house I had to leave I could watch their flight *downwards* from my window. This irrelevant detail reminds me of how animals keep all their charm, their *human* charm one might say, in our old age.

All is movement, visible or invisible, opening of buds or drooping of flowers – the petals that have fallen or the hurrying spearheads of the corn. The growth of plants, so seemingly static under a townsman's glances, is – in age's leisurely observation – one swift sinuous curve from earth to earth, birth and death and the seedling life renewed; and the trees in their small tips feel the far tremors of earth when a wandering wind drifts by. How strange to fear the Unknown which every blade of grass encounters – its possibilities so infinite, its danger merely darkness!

Countrymen have been familiar with these relationships in their youth and can find in such subtly animated and silent conversations a pleasure perhaps forgotten since childhood; but since human life too falls into the same pattern and curves with the same beauty into growth and decline (unless a hurricane tears out both plants and men), the view of this perennial harmony can be free to town or countryman alike.

Our curtain will go down when the play is ended, but we still linger among the footlights, the orchestra behind us and our eyes turned towards a country that – like the landscape round a Greek theatre – opens out from the walls of our stage. Past and future – the two preoccupations of our journey – are both in sight; and everything we see is now tinged with the strange mixture of promise and farewell. 'I am the Resurrection and the Life'; there is nothing in the world so quiet that does not symbolize this promise now so near.

The beauty of mortality is still with us, tender through imperfection and the longing it awakens to keep its passing loveliness in whatever greater majesty may come. 'What shall we remember, when we lie down?' I wrote in a very indifferent poem of my youth:

> 'the days of our childhood,
> the river gleaming,
> the distant town.'

It may be so, but there is more to it than that.

For the familiar outlines have taken on a temple atmosphere, their steps and pillars are flanking our sunset gateway on the edge of our world. Because we are all explorers, the gateway beckons, and the Unknown beyond it, while the vain beloved background of earth pours its memories, its multitudinous small moments into the short evening light. They flit like a troop of butterflies towards their last horizon, old journeys and familiar faces and childhood landscapes under the gate of Time, and old age – pausing on its way – can choose and see again perhaps Ararat rising from smooth and level ranges, or the boats, the little *grigris* from ancient Methymna, setting out for their night's fishing, with a lamp at each prow, into their mountain-shadowed sea.

The nobility of Man is in the certainty of his defeat in mortal life: there is no success attainable beyond that of a graceful death, which illuminates with the same light the hopefulness of childhood and the courage of age – one knowing, the other not knowing, that they are doomed. It is their *fragility* that ennobles them. Buildings too admit the universal weakness by pitting their strong walls and resilient lines against Time – while a poor and ugly building will pretend that its flimsy foundations can stand against the mortal tide. It is this untruth-fulness which jars. Time in them is visible only as a menace, not accepted; they try to disguise it, and their rigidity is the denial of change.

But the buildings that have adapted themselves to their mortality are enriched by Time. Their very crumbling is an emblem of life and brings to mind the inevitability of the mortal defeat – which is the measure of human courage, and awakens ad-miration and pity in the spectator.

Rocks too, in solitary places, often show the human fragility against the strength of nature: while new buildings, in their effort to deny or disguise these facts, stand in a dumb denial of the very meaning of life itself.

F. S. from a diary 18.11.60

Interlude

THE TERRESTRIAL LANDSCAPE

The Terrestrial Landscape*

It was with clearer eyes
To see all creatures full of deities.
TRAHERNE: 'Centuries'

PLEASURE IN LANDSCAPE has diminished during the last hundred years. One can say it without being a faddist for the past, and allow that some sentimentality entered into the Victorian cult of sunsets. Sentiment, and the crayons held far too tightly, informed their minute sketch books, bound in dark green with leather corners, small enough to be carried in the female reticule or the young man's pocket, and filled with innocent waterfalls, lakes, mountains – for which an appropriate foreground of muleteer or milkmaid must be found, dressed usually in dark red.

One looks at these often stilted efforts with enjoyment, and is aware of an atmosphere that lasted from crinoline to spoon-bonnet and bustle – from Jane Austen to Trollope – a rhythm of life that cultivated landscape with a number of other leisurely pursuits, and dotted it with vistas and follies and an ornamental wildness we still find delightful, though we no longer cultivate a Nature so deliberately natural. It has gone, even more completely than the studied eighteenth-century artifice that preceded its semi-emancipation. Yet these periods of urban refinement, in spite of their conventions, knew their countryside more familiarly, I imagine, than we know ours – merely from the fact that they often had to walk.

* This 'Interlude' first appeared in the author's *Space, Time and Movement in Landscape* (published in 1969 as a limited edition by her godson, the Hon. Simon Lennox Boyd, 17 Ormond Yard, London S.W.1.).

Interlude

I grew up later, in Devonshire in the furrow of the Victorians, before the first motor cars were able to face our sharply tilted hills. I can remember how one had to step out beside the pony carriage to ease the horses as they put their heads down and breasted the slope. The reins loose in one hand, while their necks bobbed up and down beside us and a sticky sucking noise accompanied the extraction of each horse-shoe from the mud, one had time to grow familiar with every fern, leaf, flower or lichen of the earth-built hedges in whose trough of shelter we trudged, and listened to the south-west soughing of the wind above us in the few bent trees that grew from the hedge's top.

The pony would stop at gateways, thinking its own thoughts as we looked out over distances that climbed from small West Country Celtic fields to the open moor. There we would see our weather, approaching or receding in spaces ample for the enjoyment of the sky – and the detail beside us and the farther reaches would become involved in the contemplation of neighbours' crops or grazing, so varied in the short stretch between the 'in-country' and the moorland.

All this complex made our 'country', and we came to know it as one knows one's own limbs, with an awareness of their possibilities but without any particular notice of their shape. And the reading of the romantics – for we were brought up on Walter Scott and Wordsworth, Keats and Shelley – though it threw its glamour over our adolescence and no doubt added its iridescent light to what we saw, was an addition to and not a substitution for the basic knowledge which came naturally to all whose business carried them from one village to the next in the long ages before the combustion engines were invented, to rivet the attention of mankind.

I was brought to think of these things through a few sentences written by Mr C. M. Butcher in *The Art News and Review* of 26 June 1958. The world, he says, as we know it now, is an image dangerously distorted by 'romantic aesthetic selection', that makes us blind 'to the realities of today upon which the future must grow'. He protests in fact against the pathetic fallacy; and perhaps, as regards the nineteenth century, he may be right. In that comfortable age, the people who wrote about landscape or painted it looked through windows solidly built; they had leisure and superfluity for passing fashions.

Yet mood is in some sort a reality, expressing permanent things with elements that are stronger than fashion. It passes through a physical impact into the imagination, and comes into landscape as a visitor, or an enhancement. The chief three among these enhancers I take to be Space, Movement and Time; and of these the first two must have appealed to the human race from its earliest existence, and perhaps even before that to animals, for dogs and horses will respond to the sweep of an open snowfield or the swiftness of a run. We cannot ask after or recapture the ecstasies of primitive man (though it would sometimes be fun, putting twos and twos together, to try to do so); even the modern countryman is inarticulate and the pleasure of a vista is supposed to pass him by; the ancient Greeks, we are told, were not interested in scenery as such. In their ripeness they had landscape fashions, but if we are looking for something more spontaneous it is in records of their youth that we find it, surviving in legend and sparkling in morning brightness – a mist left over from a forgotten night.

Landscape pervades the Greek legends, if we look into the matter with some imagination. How remarkable, how inspired – we are always being told – is the siting of their myths: and what is that but a sensitivity to landscape? We need no Victorian training to feel serenity under the pines of Olympia, across whose shallow hills and open valleys they branch a horizontal peace; or to recognize, where the cliff of Delphi hangs under the brow of Parnassus, that we are in the immediate presence of the gods. Matthew Arnold saw the Muses where moonlight drenches Helicon and anyone can see them, for the place itself, so lifted, curved, and open, so bare to the stars climbing or setting, is a link not too precipitous or sombre in its remoteness for their ideal intercourse with men.

These, Mr. Butcher may say, are the ideas of nineteenth-century highbrows, brought from Greece and perpetuated by innumerable pilgrims; their continuity through the ages still gives us our bias of today. But there are many legends tucked away in less visited places – and some of the best of them in Asia Minor, where few people have ever thought about them at all. Sleep still hangs about the silences of Latmos where the sanctuary of Endymion lies in moonlit walls and ruins far below. The wastes of Bellero-phon's madness have changed their contours with the action of the rivers of Cilicia, but their geography of desolation is the same. In the hills near Pergamon, in one of the stony valleys, the legend placed the trees that were Philemon and Baucis, and the interlacing branches of the old loving couple could be recognized and remembered, transmuted in that naked country by the gods.

Numbers of the best legends come from these lonely places where the landscape must be much as it was when they began. The Marsyas river coils in curious gorges, and one might still think to hear among the eroded rocks the flute of Asia defeated by Apollo. Where the lazy hills decrease in voluptuous folds to the Halicarnassian bay, the nymph Salmacis caught a mortal in the small lake where she lived, and prayed that their love might never be disentangled – so inventing the hermaphrodite, according to the Greeks. The gentle Aegean tinges their legends where it touches; the dark summits of Ida also have their spells; and the Black Sea bewitched the early mariners with all its strength: the mood of the present in all these regions is illustrated by their legendary past.

The Terrestrial Landscape

These tales are landscape personified, framed in remoteness and time. Invented by emotion in places that have scarcely changed, the physical powers that created them are still perceptible – lesser gods moving between earth and heaven, casting their lights and shadows on our sphere.

Apart from events, which are themselves a part of time, the triad of Time, Space and Movement chiefly produces these enhancements. They create the moods which the landscape-lover adapts to the fashion of himself or of his day; which the poet recognizes and the shepherd weaves into his tale; and the simple city man let loose in open spaces feels in the dim stir of his heart something just beyond the edge of the familiar, and yet his own.

*   *   *

SPACE

> Rather than words comes the thought of high windows;
> The sun-comprehending glass,
> And beyond it, the deep blue air that shows
> Nothing, and is nowhere, and is endless.
>
> PHILIP LARKIN: High Windows*

Some years ago I dreamed a disturbing dream. I was dead and found myself, on the far side of the living world, stepping into a lift, behind a neat, plump, and official woman in uniform. I noticed with some misgiving that the lift when it started began to go down, and continued to do so for a long way, past floor after floor of an out-door shaft among dingy houses. Their brick was decayed and their walls were undecorated except by streaks of gutters or of rain. When we reached the bottom, which was a narrow space with a few anaemic grasses imprisoned in its walls,

---

* Quoted by courtesy of the author, Faber & Faber Ltd., and Farrar, Straus & Giroux, Inc.

the conductress took up my suitcase, led the way into a mean corridor, opened the door of a small room with bed and cupboard unmitigated by anything except one of those coco-fibre mats that have always been my aversion, and saying: "Well, here you are", left me to myself. I looked to the window – uncurtained – and saw that there was no view: only a blank wall (I must have been reading Sartre). Realizing that this was my prospect for eternity, it reflects something of my natural optimism that I murmured (in my dream): "One must make the best of it I suppose", and mercifully woke up. The delight and importance of Space, my first enhancement of landscape, has remained vivid in my mind ever since.

Though Time cannot have existed in the garden of Eden, Space seems to be one of those delights that Adam and Eve could know before they came here. It is necessary as breathing. In Mussolini's north African concentration camps the Bedouin died from mere confinement. They had become a part of the width they roamed in, and the loss of it cut off their own existence as if by an amputation too drastic for their strength. And I think that in the long annals of cruelty one of the meanest acts was that of the 'White Snake', the Mogul Aurungzebe, when he bricked up the window whence his imprisoned father used to look out over the rich prolific plain of Agra and watch the life of earth to which, even in captivity, we belong.

Some people – perhaps through heredity, or timidity, or undetected fears – find security in the feeling of walls; but to me – as one can see by my dream – they are an unrelieved restriction, and the landscape of my old age is now becoming so fragile and luminous that earth and heaven run into each other unconfined as I have seen the Etruscan hills stretch to the coast of Civitavecchia and fade into the morning sun. It seems to me natural to feel transfigured in the sight of Distance, as if the shining skyline were a chalice offered by the whole world on the rounded earthly summit of its days, and oneself a part of the general invocation.

Light has a great share in this magic, light in all its changes, and who would ever forget, from some caique on the Aegean, its hour before the dawn? When the day's noise of the waves among their bubbles of foam is over, globular like the noise of doves; and the moonlight is over too, whipping with yellow thongs among the streaks of darkness, interleaving their shadows, or cradling in the ship's wake the bunches of rosy foam round the coasts of Cythera, as if the footsteps of Aphrodite were printed on the sea?

But the hour before the dawn is colourless, shining like a waiting mirror among the Cyclades, in the only sea that is lighter than its sky. The light when it comes casts over it a gossamer yellow veil, a film of day. The sky is quiescent; the transformation is all in the water: when the sun rises the horizon vanishes in the general blankness, all is liquid white. An increase of radiance alone shows the sea with feathers of colour, that form and vanish in wide undinted undulations smooth as sleep.

But when the sun is high enough to look down, the water darkens to sapphire, and sun and sea glitter to each other and the sky is forgotten: and perhaps the whole Greek feeling of the divinity of man is in this supremacy of the ocean, a response of earth so much greater than the skyey benediction that created it? For man here was a god and made the heavens seem small in his frail vessel, lit by the sun that waked him in his dawn: it was under darker and stronger skies of Italy and Europe that he was once again brought into subjection to the humanity of heaven.

The caique meanwhile continues and is still queen in her own waters in spite of steam. She uses oil now in the lop-sided cabin on her thwarts; an electric bulb carelessly lit hangs from her mast in the daylight; and her colours are bleached but gay – that daffodil yellow, that turquoise, the red like Chinese lacquer, the pomegranate black, the happy edgings and splashings of her sides – in their mellowness among the Pontic breezes and catspaw shadings she still points East through Marmara for Byzantium–Istanbul.

She is laden not to the gunwale but beyond it – the sand or figs or barrels in her hold kept dry only by a plank or two casually nailed to keep the waves out. Everything else in the sea moves faster than she does. She is so loaded that she ought to sink but does not, and some splendid accident must have presided over her shape to make it last so long. Wide-waisted and low, with pointed prow and rising stern, antique, overburdened, patched and scurried round by newer speeds, she keeps the majesty of the Greco-Roman civilization that has made her and us; and the seagulls with wings like eyebrows hover round her, leaning motionless sideways in the current of the air, as if in a ballet, with cool invisible dancing art.

In her day the saying was invented that it is better to voyage hopefully than to arrive, and this is the meaning of Space. To arrive is immobility and death, a thing that must never happen to one's heart, whatever the poor body may be doing; and the first axiom to remember in all travel or books of travel is that every horizon has a horizon beyond it, that every journey's end is a stage in another journey, and that the final immobility – if it is stationary at all – is so far beyond our perception that it is safer to look upon it in the light of a direction rather than a goal.

Space is in fact, in landscape, the element of the unseen. By its presence it tells us of what is not there. In a documentary age it is the antidote to the crowd of facts – too many and full of danger and misleading, apart from being suggestive of arrival which disturbs the genuine traveller, and unpleasant like the slamming of a door in one's face.

Space is the nothing, the interval, the silence.

Until recently, mystery was spontaneous in a world

where so little was known. The universe stood in its ordered theatre with infinity and eternity behind it, and everything was on an edge of danger and delight: and to some, and I think they are the fortunate, this is still so. It should be so, one imagines, to scientists whose world has leaped into immensity, though they live too far beyond the average scope to be generally articulate about it. Yet it may not be so. The sense of mystery belongs to what we do not know and disappears when we concentrate on what we do know. It is the step beyond the horizon, the trail of the cloud, the footstep of wind. It is the most transporting among the enhancements of landscape, with a Dionysiac quality that acts like wine, or like some clarifying drug increasing human power: for we are if we wish it everything that our sight can embrace or our conception imagine; our seeing makes us so, and every emptiness on the horizon makes us free of a world beyond.

*   *   *

TIME

> Take to the everlasting
> All that time has taught.
> SIEGFRIED SASSOON: 'Resurrection, March 1948'

Time in landscape may be described as the vertical of space. It can burrow, deep as you please, where space is narrow, through layer upon layer of our past. To feel it is to enlarge the world's compass not once or twice but a thousand-fold, to the boundaries of knowledge, where Time will take us into solitudes no tourist-crowd disturbs. It can move swiftly through the millennia of geology, or slowly through the deviousness of men. The most intimate of the enhancements of landscape, it brings the universe and all that has made it into our very being – a part of what, at this moment, we are; and to be deaf to its subdued perpetual, ubiquitous eloquence is to listen to the symphony of life with some of the deepest notes missing.

When I first became aware of Time I must have been very small – perhaps six years old. Our land ran into Dartmoor and held in its heathery edges stone circles where people brought flocks and lived through forgotten summers before the Romans came. In the daytime I would play in and out of the boulders they had propped up to make their houses; but when dusk crept with mists from the upper moors, I would walk round in the deep heather and avoid the grassy centres of their floors; they were inhabited, I felt, and not to be disturbed.

The whole moor was very old – the oldest rock in England, my father told me. On the tors, whose granite lay in folded slabs like triple or quadruple chins, the wind scoured small rock pools in which pebbles were blown round and round, widening their prison through the imperceptible aeons of their labour. I would sit watching them, listening to the thin voices of the wind. Everything was hard there: the moss, brittle and dark and close, like the black weave dyed with pomegranate or walnut skin in Persian rugs; or jade-green, bearing upright cups a dewdrop would drown. And the stone itself, minutely faceted in colours, bright but here subdued, was compacted into an unyielding glaze for its long weather war. The awareness of Time, of the endless attrition of the wheel that is us since we are turning with it, came to me naturally, as it can never come to children in a city, where the universal quality of the procession is not seen.

Years later, by

> The tideless dolorous midland sea,
> In a land of sand, and ruin, and gold
> SWINBURNE

where Time is almost supreme, its eloquence seemed familiar: I had long ago met these voices in my childhood.

It must not be thought that the discovery of Time in a landscape is a mere matter of ruin and decay. It is not the end, but the transitions that enthrall us – transformations that have no visible frontiers in future or in past. The works of men share in the universal discipline and are harmonious as they are subject to the general law of ruin: they are displeasing when they seem to claim a permanence which is not theirs by nature: the builder, modern as he may be, must remain aware that the world he steps into is fluid as a stream. Beyond this awareness, he shares the privilege of every other art, and may step across the temporal barrier if he can; for something is to be found in this world which is of its essence everlasting, and the noblest ruins weave immortality in their decline.

While the matter lasts which he moulded – while even a fragment remains – the footprint of the great architect or artist is that of a victor across the sands of Time.

Part II

THE MIRROR OF SHALOTT

I

A Dialogue on Age

To the many Gods
Libations pour with which to venerate
The Unity supreme.
>   *The Temple*. Arthur Waley trans.

>   The land of life to look at and explore –
>   Is this, then, to grow old?
>   SIEGFRIED SASSOON. 'Euphrosy', 1949

YOU MUST IMAGINE a party of four on a summer's night, dining on the rough terrace of a small *trattoria*. It overlooks the Venetian plain whose lights shine with a harder brilliance as the industrializing of Italy progresses, but they are spread along roads now emptied under a softer moon, and a country quietness lies around. In the pleasant silence, with good wine on the table, there is nothing to complain of except Drusilla, engaged in a crusading war against parents in general and hers in particular, into which a long tirade against old age is marshalled. The party is not too well chosen – elderly to old apart from Drusilla, who would have been left at home with a book in my far years of youth if my parents happened to be enjoying themselves alone: but now that family life is becoming conscientious, Drusilla has been listened to almost from her baby years and has become impervious to signs of boredom; and we went home early in a jaded frame of mind. Thinking over the evening and its implications, I built up this argument in a pseudo-Socratic way, for my own amusement.

"Dear girl," my imaginary self observed, to a Drusilla a good deal more amenable than the reality, "It seems to me that you are reasoning in a circle, and your dislike of old age and – unhappily for us – old people, is being repeated very often without working towards any constructive end. Supposing we look into the matter more soberly to discover what can be said on either side? You can begin, and give me three points in your argument, and I will take up the defence as best I can and try to contradict them: and then I will do the same in the defence of age and you shall contradict if you like and can." "Why yes," said Drusilla, "I can easily do that." "Yes indeed," said I, "but you must make your points short and clear, with neater edges than you trimmed them with at dinner. Now begin with the chief of them."

"Well," said she, with a new sort of amiability which showed how useful it is to put people on their mettle. "Well, I should begin by complaining of the *fixed* quality of age. As its body stiffens, so does its mind, and we young people are faced with rules, ideas and convictions far behind our time but which, whether we agree with them or not, can never be altered."

"A reasonable complaint," said I. "What is your second?"

"My second," said Drusilla after pondering for a minute or so, "is that these fixed ideas are not only used by the old for themselves, which would not matter, but are clamped on to us like a sort of cage so that either we have to stay inside and agree, or break out with much-criticized violence."

"That makes two points," said I, "and it seems to me they are well-chosen. Now what is your third complaint?"

Drusilla had no hesitation over this point. "It is the *feebleness* of old age which makes it unbearable to the young," she said. "Not only do we have to put up with the old, but we have to be sorry for them, and when we are impatient we find our consciences filled with remorse. I think these are my three main points," she concluded.

"Well," I said, "I am not going to dispute your first point, or say, as one often hears it said, that these fixed opinions of old are the wisdom of life gradually distilled. Sometimes they are and sometimes – wisdom being rare – more usually they are not, so we will leave them for the time being and I shall base my defence against both your first points on something quite different – and namely on the claim that this *fixity* imposed on you is not a matter to be dealt with at all by the old, but rather by the young themselves: for the old – when their minds are once fixed – are obviously incapable of dealing with a matter for which *elasticity* is the only remedy: and this particular virtue must be provided by youth."

"But what can we do," said Drusilla, "except quite uselessly protest?"

"You can do everything," I said, "but you must do it before you become old, for the benefit, if not for yourself, then for your children. I will put it to you in a simile – that of a road, for instance, which has the habit of breaking down in some difficult spot: one would not expect the actual traveller when he reaches it to repair it, nor blame him if he finds it difficult to cross: one would criticize a want of interest long before when something could have been foreseen and mended. Now this fixed condition of the old both in mind and body is a break of this kind and no sudden or surprising event, but is something that sooner or later freezes all mortal roads and could have been fore-seen. When the disaster happens it is too late to do any-thing about it, since the capacity itself for change has gone. We all know that this is bound to happen; there is no surprise about it and it is one of the accidents we can be most sure of in this world: the breaking up of our road's surface is therefore a thing to be thought about in time – before forty, or even thirty, let us say – since elasticity becomes ever more difficult from quite an early age. It is you, my dear Drusilla, young as you are now, who can see to it that by discipline and constant attention to your own condition your children may be spared the disappointment which your imprudent parents have provided for you."

Drusilla received this advice with a rather discontented expression.

"I don't see how this helps me personally very much," she said at last.

"That," said I, "is because, if you wish to be agreeably adaptable in your old age, your education should have taken quite a new slant from the beginning: it should be an exercise in *giving* rather than *taking*, and the pleasures of giving – service and love and all-day virtues – would have to take the place of a number of other pleasures. I have often thought of this when visiting in Turkey, where the women are trained to be amiable; it makes a most livable though slightly one-sided family atmosphere, and one may notice there that, if the constant practice of amiability is not able to destroy the rigidity of age, it does at least modify its expression. If you ponder on this, my dear Drusilla, you will see that your children, if not you, could escape most of the sufferings which your two first complaints describe.

"As for the third – the feebleness and helplessness of age – although that indeed is incurable in itself, it can be welcomed as a training ground for your own pleasure in *giving* – so much more conveniently practised among relatives near at hand than among the poor in remote places where philanthropy is quite liable to do harm."

Drusilla's three points were now left as it were to stew in their own juice and we turned to what might be said, in a less negative way, in Age's favour.

"For my first point," I said, "I would ask you to notice that in the fervour of a progressive age we are forgetting the importance of looking back as well as forward. We may again take the simile of a road, or rather of a path in the hills where, in its uncertain moments, every mountaineer would pause to look over the way he had travelled, so as to make sure of his forward direction. In life, the same necessity arises, and looking back, whether on lives or philosophies or buildings, is the *only* means we have to ascertain the direction that has carried us so far and is to take us on. It is the forward glance in reverse, and old age is our only document for obtaining it. The Past – a treasure house for the old – is, or should be, a springboard for the young, to push them on along their way with a knowledge of what lies behind them.

"This is my first point, and as for my second, I would choose the very feebleness and helplessness you complain of, and add even the faults of old age: for all these offer as it were a training ground to produce that readiness to give with everyday amiability which I have tried to describe to you as your chief instrument for happiness when your own old age comes in its turn."

"And what is your third point?" says Drusilla not at all convinced.

"Well," said I, "the qualities that we have hitherto criticized or admired depend on circumstances or on other people rather than on the independent choice of Age: but for my last and chiefest point I would select Discrimination, a virtue that the old can practise if they wish. Some have it and others not, but it is essential if age is to become bearable at all. Why do the egotists, so attractive and good looking when young, become so boring? Because they are interested in something that does not interest other people – in themselves; and the young, who can have the world for their horizon, will not spend much time peering into a little dusky cell full of worries: they will by-pass, if they can, the prose of middle age that may often clutter up the interests of their parents, and look perhaps to their grandparents on the threshold of a timeless climate that belongs to all.

This climate is fundamentally common and therefore interesting to every age of man. Its horizon is vaster than the skyline of youth. It lies close to the aged, beyond their limits of space or time and it is youth's future also: so that the old people's way of facing or considering it with the avenue of their past to guide them must ever be of common interest, an example or a warning. Their road opens beyond their own bitter or interrupted places, whose minor incidents and momentary troubles should never be allowed to distract them completely from this great climax to which every life sinks or rises; and in their later years the discrimination of the old should be directed to the timelessness of life. In that common adventure youth and age can feel themselves companions on the road."

Surprisingly enough Drusilla, who is an honest girl, agreed. "If I could do so, I should still not wish to demolish your points," she said, "particularly the last."

But of course it is merely a dialogue invented by myself.

2

The Mirror of Shalott

The strength failing sooner than the song
PLINY on the nightingale

MANY YEARS AGO, when I was I suppose sixteen or
seventeen, I saved enough money through months of
economy to buy Skeat's Etymological Dictionary. This
cherished possession, extremely heavy to lift and, one
would imagine, to assimilate, was for quite a long time my
treasured companion. Words flourished in its ponderous
pages in their own atmosphere, half-buried in abbrevia-
tions: they carried their travels about them and – often
misused and miserable among us – began to show me
what innate majesty belonged to their long sojourn in the
minds of men.

They began in fact to *speak* and, as far as I am concerned,
have never lost the enchantment with which the Rev.
Doctor invested them. Dedicating his volume 'to the
suppression of such guesswork as entirely ignores all rules',
he believed that the study of language, 'frequently
complicated by the interference of one word with another
. . . can yet be pursued in a spirit of reverence similar to
that in which we study what are called the works of
nature.'

In my last essay in this volume I have tried to express the
belief that many, perhaps most of our sorrows today and
for tomorrow are due to our misuse of and contempt for
words; nor can I ever be grateful enough for my first
acquaintance with them not as dead objects to be thrown
around promiscuously, but as living essences, travellers

from age to age, from nation to nation, precise and light-footed dancers in and out of the meanings of man.

This discovery has given a constant delight to my life. It is extended in old age not to words only but to almost everything that we can hear or see. In youth the rapture hit one in a straightforward way – the Alps outstretched, or Venice on the water, the creeping winds or blossoming trees transparent in the sun – each little hammerstroke awakened its separate response. But in age it is as if every separate note contains in itself all variety of quality or distance, so that the most inconsiderable experience may lose itself and be – as the doctor said – 'complicated by the interference of another' – not necessarily a word, but a sight, or a scent, or happiness or sorrow; the thing in itself is not itself only, but a part of the accumulation that it and we have made.

Age is thus assailed by a thousand remembered horizons, and the appearance of a view or a mere tree or stream or thought can bring with it a thousand differing or similar trees or streams, each with their trail of circumstance around them. In this profusion the sharpness of outline is impaired, and youth may feel puzzled or impatient with such vagueness in what itself sees so sharply cut and clear. The difference however is fundamental: youth looks *at* its world and age looks *through* it; youth must get busy on problems whose outlines stand single and strenuous before it, while age can, with luck, achieve a cosmic private harmony unsuited for action as a rule. If these two activities are wrongly timed, trouble arises – youth having dealt with its problems too little, with nothing much left to blend in future years, and age in its over-furnished room musing that it may yet recapture the naked separateness of facts that in their temporal way created action.

We are sitting, in our old age, with the mirror of Shalott before us on the doorstep of eternity. Our story has already begun to merge with other stories, peacefully or painfully breathing with the breathing of earth. Within and beyond us everywhere is the divine Unity free of Time and Space, the everlasting. And without that harmony, with death soon coming, what is man but a castaway on a small rock with a rising tide?

This is the fear of death.

Yet the divine is alive in us by whatever name we call it, a thread however slender, a particle of eternity in the concourse of Time. It is *us* – that which, known or unknown, makes us immortal, and, by whatever name we call it, is alive within us, it is *us*.

It is well, while we leave the young to their tasks, at our end and their beginning, that – novices as we are – we listen to what even in our own world is already taking us some way out of Time. Death there is but a stepping stone, where Space itself has faded among what cannot fade, even if our planet sink. Because of this, our foresight of eternity, we are entitled to set our frontiers upon a timeless ground.

3

Tradition

And late man, listening through his latter grief
Hears, close or far, the oldest of his joys,
Exactly as it was, the water noise.
AUDEN: 'The Shield of Achilles'

I SOMETIMES REMEMBER Kipling's poem 'If'. It hung, neatly typed in a frame, on the wall of a white-washed living-room in Baghdad, scantily furnished as they were in those bare days – for this was 1942 and German armies were advancing from north and west.

The room belonged to a youngish man and talented musician, the Sherif Mohedin Haidar Ali, whose brother, also a good friend of mine, was helping with Cairo's growing committees in our Egyptian Brotherhood of Freedom. Both were sons of H. H. the Sherif Ali Haidar, Emir of Mecca from 1916 to 1923, the holiest functionary of Islam. After a life of great honour and goodness, and when left a widower with three sons, he had married Miss Isobel Dunn, who had long devoted herself to the education of these children. She became H. H. Princess Fatma and lived for many years in quiet happiness in the retirement required at that time even in Istanbul by the Sherif's religious eminence and the holiness of Mecca. After his death she settled in Beirut, and was in Cairo when I was there; and to my regret the meeting I had hoped for was prevented by the agitations of war. All I could realize was the singular sweetness and steadfastness of this woman, of whom her stepson, Muhammad Amin, always spoke with the greatest affection.

I saw less of the Sherif Mohedin, but one day he took me across his white-washed room to where 'If' hung on the wall: "I guide my life by it", he said.

The other remembrance I have of this poem belongs to the years of the war when our defeats in Arakan and Burma were taking their heavy toll. Lord Wavell (then C.-in-C., India, and in command) after some poor sorrowful stumbling words of mine, quoted the lines:

> 'If you can meet with triumph and disaster
> And treat those two impostors just the same,'

he said, with his direct gaze.

The poem is not the greatest verse, but it keeps its values; an Arab and an Englishman of that day could use it as the measure for their lives because, in its song, it expresses a tradition, slowly filtered from sonorous roots and distant sources, the water of our proper stream. Tradition speaks with fibres alive but forgotten, built into our being as a protection more redoubtable than armies, good for uncounted resistences, unrecorded upheavals, alliances, or revolts as the impeded current may direct.

Those born into it are apt to forget that its secret is one of *steady and unceasing motion*. If arrested, revolution follows – revolution which is merely accelerated movement usually made destructive by frustration, but in itself a part of tradition, a hitch in its continuity, a beating of foam against some obstacle in the bedrock of the stream, which the statesman in his past should have foreseen and avoided.

Identical qualities in different forms come again and again to its surface. In the long tradition of Britain there is a constantly visible dislike of surveillance, a reluctance to be managed, a preference for one's own inventive strain. Anglo-Saxon poets, Piers Plowman, Malory, Shakespeare show this idiosyncrasy and it makes its way through the foreign fashions of the Renaissance into the age of Napoleon and our day.

Tradition

Our welfare state, which was a generous and spontaneous effort when it came, should have remembered this, and clinging to our traditional minimum of administration, should more successfully and with all its heart have avoided above all things the surveillance of bureaucracy as peculiarly unsuited to our climate. Strikingly excluded from centuries of public and parliamentary life, and reluctantly admitted only when the necessities of two wars made it in some measure essential, bureaucracy contradicts about two thousand years of a history whose burgesses and bishops, lords and squires and pilgrims lifted civilization across much medieval wildness to our southern shores.

We have lost our empire, and the most precious thing lost with it was an easy freedom for *initiative* open to the whole youth of Britain. It disappeared in the slice of a generation, and there are few yet who feel happy to tot up their lives with computers instead. In a fundamental way this might not matter: nations have been poor and brave and happy, cutting their furrow through a promiscuous world. But bureaucracy is not *our* way of doing it, and through all the clamour of advertisement, television, radio, press and the urgent call of economics, the slowly built-up character remains.

It will move, but in its own direction. It must always, I may repeat, be kept imperceptibly moving, and the statesman's business is to see that it does so; its future must be aligned with the whole surprising length of its past. Gaps of misery in most histories show the periods when this harmonious progress was contradicted, either by alien conquest or by native blindness, and the discord had to work itself out in disorder – penury or rebellion or suppression – according to the legislation of its day.

The stress has been mitigated in England on the whole by a certain natural fairness of character, not heroic but lazy and lovable, which in a divergence is often able to see the other side as clearly as its own. It kept the miracle of our improvised empire alive for as long as it lasted, and is a quality particularly valuable in those who govern, whatever their starting point may be; for it can stimulate them to undertake their own discomfort – a thing which our history has often shown to happen. Such revolutions spurred from below but accomplished from above – in good time and with only reasonable disturbance – have been a hallmark and speciality of the English tradition, inherited both from Roman and barbarian.

Old age, which is supposed to be traditional and now interests me more than politics, has a natural rigidity. Its landscape is so nostalgic that any movement can spoil it, and though there are veterans who remain rather boisterously at one with the young, they too share a natural reaction against changes that show the passing of Time too vivid and too near. Only when the still-active years have dwindled into leisure, and past and present begin to drift into one distance and lose not their significance but their sharpness – then only can age enjoy a pleasure hitherto neglected or unobserved; and seated above the battle like Xerxes on his throne, can see its own steps marked or forgotten below, and the world's river with our small tributaries inside it winding to the sea. In its sunny or shady patches it still can find its own suns and shadows, and feel the unity of Time as old countrymen know it walking home through their harvests, or craftsmen who see in their last efforts the hopes and aspirations of their youth. We look on at young sails now set to meet their new uncharted breezes, and at our country's vessel stuffing paper into its leaking sides; and beyond the falling night a dawn is preparing as usual, secret and strange in the East.

Charm of Naples that it *is* the Hellenistic world – decayed, but inside its own tradition. It is what all these little objects, these terra-cotta figures and gay smooth marble and ivory, these cups and ear-rings and ornamental armours were leading to in their rich precarious world. It is what *we* are going towards . . . all in the same direction though with lessened gaiety. Worlds of profusion – what can prevent their decay? A rigid pursuit of excellence? The constant recognition that this ease of living is *secondary* . . . Naples is the Greco-Roman world, with the conviction that made it taken away: the cleverness with no purpose becomes slickness: yet the same Hellenistic ability appears.

Poignant little scene: a man selling toy tortoiseshell violins: "It makes music" he says, putting one to his ear and his eyes lighten with pleasure. They have kept the gift – to love 'what makes music' in the disinterested Greek fashion. With their touches of gaiety, their resentment of dullness, they throw a gossamer to cover their abyss.

F. S. from a diary 26.9.60

4

Pleasures of Age

It *has* all by other means than *having*, for what it possesses is still Itself.

PLOTINUS

It sufficeth that he who is unable to give shall be willing to receive.

ST BASIL, Letter CLI

THERE IS NO DOUBT THAT, after eighty, the number of our pleasures declines. Someone remarked many years ago how brave it was of M. Clemenceau to shoot tigers in India (when about seventy as far as I remember). This seemed to me nonsense at the time, and continues to do so now, with one year less to lose as each year passes: if it gave pleasure and one disliked tigers, why not shoot them if one can? But yet, though the horizon opens with age, the possibility of exploring it decreases, and tiger-shooting is one of the things one is inclined to drop.

Among the pleasures that can be continued and even begun after eighty the best, it seems to me, is *sharing*. The Arabs, until goaded into a Western attitude, believed in this virtue (in a casual way), and even their beggars have always considered that it is the bestower who is lucky. In the West, where property has a dragon clutch, the approach to generosity is made easier by age, and helps us to comfort the melancholy of departure. Wrapped softly and remotely in a serenity which should be the climax of all our striving, our minds follow those trinkets which our life has gathered, objects from days and years so full of loves and tumults, floating in new hands into a new sunrise where they will be happy and we may be remembered. This can generally be done only in fancy, for we keep a few odds and ends around us till we go: but the parting should already be made in the heart.

Yet it seems to be a toss-up whether we become lavish or stingy and one or other of these undesirable fates is more or less predestined with age. Like a small skiff with an obstacle in sight and the current against it, we do what we can to redress the balance: but the current originated in childhood years ago; the carefulness or rashness of ancestors find themselves in our latest ledgers; and what we look at with satisfaction or dismay, according to our prudence or irresponsibility, is a foregone conclusion.

The modern trend is against giving as a whole, though philanthropy is in the ascendant. We are coming to look at human beings more and more in groups and categories, while the sharing-happiness is one of individuals and of love; and it is a poor present that does not offer as much pleasure, or more, to giver than receiver. Good works, getting mass-produced, are coming to be unwillingly provided, with little warmth between those who extract and those who bestow: and irrelevant things like Xmas cards or stamps have to be found to give an illusion of investment to the noble act of giving.

This is usually looked upon as kindness towards others – generosity to our 'proximity' as the Italians rather nicely call it – but it is in reality ourselves that we benefit with gifts. The procession *moves*, we must remember; we have added to its riches or its poverty the stuff itself with which the Past has built us: the whole of it, mostly unrecognized or unknown, clarifies or pollutes the future stream and our contribution, small or great, is all that life has done with us and all we have to give. The Future now has our skein to unravel and the Three Sisters with their one eye between them are at it already, disentangling good or bad. In the frozen climate of age we must continue to walk for a little while in our direction as happily as we can. "If a tortoise," says Plotinus, "is caught in a procession and moving the wrong way, it will get trodden on." Beloved Plotinus, always right. One can turn, and cause discomfort to one's neighbours, or walk straight trusting to oneself, but one is usually in a regiment, or a group, or a rabble, once young and now becoming singularly old, yet furnished with convictions of its own.

In these circumstances the pleasure of sharing reaches its most delicate perceptions. It is no longer the comradeship of youth when the whole world animate and inanimate seemed to recognize our joy and our surprises; we have made our selection, and the things that move us remain just as astonishing but more deeply enduring to ourselves. There is now a more rare and costly quality about sharing them, a privacy as it were of interchange: and if it is a matter of tangible gifts, there is a warmth, as of two travellers under one cloak for a few miles of a way that threatens to grow cold.

Sharing becomes above all things a preparation for the step-over into a climate free of Space or Time, where property is not. It proves that small trickle of human solidarity which has survived the world's ill-treatment and is so deeply moving in the history of men. It should come at an age when the restrictions of life can open to timeless expanses. If it is not there then, a discord, an ugliness appears – a clutch hardening on trifles as transitory (we may now discover) as petrol, and our uniform stream heading for its future is checked. The procession looks forward, and happiness, even past, if it gives pleasure no longer, must not be dwelt on with more than a passing regret.

Our small gifts carry no such anti-climax, scattered free as birds that follow the descending caravan. When the fires have sunk and the men are couched around them, and the new dawn will not find us when it breaks, these too will have flown to their new habitations with perhaps an unforgotten glint of our own friendly daylight on their wings.

5

Malignities of Age

The best thing we can do
Is to make whatever we're lost in
Look as much like home as we can.
CHRISTOPHER FRY: *The Lady's not for Burning*

AN ALMOST FORGOTTEN affair between Iraq and the
British military in 1920, an aftermath of the First
World War, was described in a book by General Sir
Aylmer Haldane, the English commander. It opens with
the climate which people who knew the country in those
days had reasons to remember: it was a good climate, he
declared, apart from the incidence of plague, cholera,
typhus, dysentery, and malaria. One might make the
same sort of statement when writing about old age,
varying the menu and balancing it with a list of its own –
of poverty, solitude, sickness, decay, and eventually of
course death: and it does not seem to me fair to describe a
time of life which I find pleasant without dealing with
these drawbacks as well: I shall leave out solitude, to
which I have dedicated an essay of its own, and death,
since we are on the whole happier with it than we could be
without it: but the other three must be examined and they
require, it seems to me, a great deal of discrimination.

Poverty, for instance. To keep, if one can, moderate
riches is natural: to want, or even resign oneself to, *great*
riches is surely foolish unless one has a mind, a genius, and
energy to make and carry out great plans. It is mostly
disappointing to see what milliardaires do with their
money and, as I write in Italy, they are spending most of it

at the moment in ransoming their kidnapped children. But even in non-revolutionary societies the labour entailed by wealth is meant for youth: after eighty, time and health are needed with perhaps enough left over to buy or do – and not too easily – some thing that life has taught us most to wish for, and with never enough to make one feel a personal almost guilty pang at the sight of poverty in others.

Walking in Tashkent when the autumn was already falling, one saw the streets being swept by the old women: *expendable*, that sad war-word seemed written on their faces, and the heat and dust of summer, and the cold of winter alone now marked their years: when I remember them, a sort of constriction catches me at the heart; those colourless eyes continue to haunt one; however efficient the world may become, I cannot think a civilization worth having that does not encourage and enable its subjects to spend something, not extorted by governments but freely given to keep wretchedness at least from the streets they walk through day by day. There are very poor lands in fierce climates where one can still knock at any door, or stop at a tent, and be fed; and in my childhood, on market days when beggars came round with their scrips, bread would never be refused, though an obviously prosperous beggar would quite often be haughty enough to disdain it. This embryonic medieval system can only flourish where poverty is familiar, and the present time is no doubt economically better for the recipient; but the other laid a trail of warmth in the hearts of *givers* through the dark uncomfortable forests of feudal Europe back to the centuries when Rome was sinking and patrician ladies were devoting their substance to the poor; and indeed long before.

Such a purely personal bond is in danger of being lost in the progress of organization, seal of our common humanity and general fate. But it was human warmth, and not the carefulness of bureaucracy that blossomed in our cathedrals and almost deserted country churches, and in those early hospitals whose beauty still civilizes the ruins of Christianity or Islam; and to old age in particular, when the world's veil grows more transparent, it seems vital that the thread of love, the essence of our united human destiny in its poor vestiges, should be preserved for *individuals* to enjoy, givers or receivers as the case may be: there is no innate divergence between them.

From poverty to sickness is a step downhill, since sickness is the more difficult for rich or poor to manage. We escape with relief from poverty's clutches – whether grabbing at us or our neighbours – and are glad of any excuse to be quit of her in our thoughts even for an hour, a month or a year or two, though the bill must be mounting up at the end; and it is noticeable that it is the well-to-do who talk about their difficulties which those more fundamentally poor are only too happy to forget.

But sickness is another matter, concerning our very citadel of peace by the simple expedient of confining us to ourselves. In that compulsion no happiness is possible: if sickness is slight, we can play with the thought of release like a prisoner behind bars: but if it is serious or fatal there is no true comfort except in escape from our identity – some window on one world or another must be opened. This has to be done in spite of loved ones, who are tilting against us with remedies, sympathies, precautions, and anxieties that clamp the living spirit to its bed and centre its attention on what is giving so much trouble at the moment. For this reason, having just recovered from an operation, I am all in favour of sickness in hospital, where gay and brisk young nurses will talk of their own affairs, like the stream of a healthy current through a swamp.

But I have been ill also in lonely places, with no one in particular to attend to me. Too weak to read – I remember those vacant days strangely, with a great arch of serenity above them as they gazed in their wide leisure on the majestic approaches of death. This is of course what must happen to sickness in age, when that visitor is liable to drop in at any moment. It is kind, I think, like a firm hostess with an unpopular guest, to welcome and make room for him without too much fuss.

Charles II apologized to his court for being 'an unconscionable time a-dying', and it is a help *in extremis* if politeness is required or if children or others as dear make selflessness a duty and our most intimate manners have to be good enough not to give pain: for the basic damage that sickness can do is to enthrone the Ego and leave self-pity to its dreary reign.

But when all is said, there are few things that can reconcile us fully to our parting with a world of which the longest life can see so little and whose beauties have so extraordinary a variety. True faith or deep unhappiness alone can see us out, and I think that the worst unpleasantness of age is not its final fact, or any discomfort we have been reciting, but the tediousness of preparation, the accumulating number of defeats. Adjustments should be made with gaiety, but it is all very slow, and one of the few civilized aspects of ancient Roman life was the composure with which one could slip out when the banquet was ended: the solidity of paganism compares rather well on this point with a Christianity that acts so differently from its own teaching.

We have seen that poverty, solitude, sickness and death all have a salutary and indeed a favourable aspect; but, perhaps because I am in the midst of it myself, there is nothing particularly pleasant I can find to say about this preliminary process of decay which cannot get much better and is likely at any moment to get worse. It hovers, like those moments in railway stations when the goodbyes are said and the train is not yet starting: and that, of course, is what it is.

The explorers (there are many of all ages) have an advantage in the fact that the thought of a frontier allures them; and the old are going where most of their loved ones have already adventured, so that the unknown goal seems as crowded as the world they are to leave: but the wrench is there, and faith is a gift of God.

I will close this unwelcome little catalogue with a dream's end that stayed when I woke up, years ago; still vivid as a picture, I wrote it out word for word at the time, because of the surprise at its conclusion.

A woman, pleasantly middle-aged, stood half-way up a ladder in a small country shop, with a shelf and some crockery above her, "and", she said, finishing our unknown conversation, "as I climbed for that yellow teapot, I saw my future clear below me – the little house, a glow of lamp, a palisade of garden, a bus or station a mile or so away (but I would not often use them), and Bill would be mostly away, going about his doings; and I would be there to welcome him coming or going, a hostess in the house of God."

I have added nothing to her words but the punctuation; and the placid little landscape, so modestly suburban, so contrasted to my vagrant life, so happy and so easily attainable in a decent world, and with its final sudden opening on to the universal, gave me then, and still gives me, the pleasant fancy that one may find oneself at home wherever or whatever one may be.

But as for the malignities of age, the answer was given by one farmer to another as they came out from some sermon which pictured their possible future in hell: "It will have to be borne," they were saying.

6

'Permissive' and the Negative Virtues

Pasan, serenas las horas, no hay guerra en el mundo
y duerme bien el labrador, viendo el cielo en el
fondo alto de su sueño.

XIMENEZ. *Platero y yo*.

OBEDIENCE, chastity, strictness of duty – respectable
virtues with a medieval ancestry, encouraged by
Dr. Arnold and flourishing under Victoria – they have
vanished underground like desert rivers and at present
show no sign of reappearing. In my own lifetime they
have become almost improper to mention – banished
in any case from the public scene and replaced after
the First World War by the poor alternative adjective
permissive.

I am not out to defend them, for they are negative in
themselves, and meant to be used only as a boundary to
retrench the vagabond lawlessness of man. The enchantment, the beauty which a virtue must have if it is to
be a virtue indeed, is borrowed: it comes to them from a
presence outside themselves, a radiance which their
fence is built to protect and defend.

> There dwells sweet love, and constant chastity,
> Unspotted faith and comely womanhood,
> Regard of honour and mild modesty;
> There virtue raynes as queen in royal throne,
> And giveth lawes alone,
> The which the base affections doe obey,
> And yield their services unto her will;

Ne thought of thing uncomely ever may
Thereto approach to tempt her mind to ill.
Had ye once seen these her celestial treasures,
And unrevealéd pleasures,
Then would ye wonder, and her prayses sing,
That al the woods should answer, and your echo ring.*

It is not possible to quarrel with words like these: but the loveliness that is so praised is not the subservient virtue but Love itself in its timeless light.

So with the other two. It is not so much Obedience as what is obeyed that has the 'integra, consonantia, claritas' – the wholeness, harmony, radiance defined by St. Thomas Aquinas. And Duty as a virtue, *stern daughter of the voice of God*, must also get her halo from outside as it were, before the *Godhead's most benignant grace* can show.

She *preserves the stars from wrong*, says Wordsworth, who overlapped into the Victorian age; and this negative touch, this quality of being a defence rather than an adventure, has robbed all the three virtues of their modern charm. To see them in their proper setting one must go back to the early Christianity when education, almost entirely monastic, was a jungle adventure surrounded by renunciations and dangers. These three were then helpful as the black and white stripes are helpful to motorists at dangerous corners: their warning kept one on the road. Like an athlete's training, their innate quality of boredom was lost in its objective, and their decline is due to the fact that the Faith which inspired and encouraged them has almost disappeared.

Far above their world, in flashes of a hidden sun, the bird of Faith was sailing in their sky. Its intimate, eternal fires lit their terrestrial efforts, their many abdications sacrificed to the inexpressible progress of light. The shadow of its wing, the safety of man's sunset in his West,

* Spenser – for his own wedding.

were the prize of these renunciations; and when the great bird sped from our geography, the virtues that were meant to ease his visitations drooped and died.

Permissive was found instead, as a substitute in the shaken conditions that followed the First World War – a word in whose poor sky the only visible wings are those of Lucifer falling through Space towards Chaos and Night

> Into this wild abyss,
> The womb of nature and perhaps her grave.*

A new fashion in adjectives is surely needed?

* *Paradise Lost*: Book, II, 910–11.

7

Leadership

If there were no sun it would be night, for all the other stars.

HERACLITUS

Hold sacred thy capacity for forming opinions.

MARCUS AURELIUS. *Meditations*.

THE BATTLE of Albuera was won by the regiment now known as the Middlesex. Their nickname – Diehard – was drawn from words repeated by their officers, walking among them on the slope that must be held: 'Die hard, men, die hard' – and so they did. In its unflinching line along the shallow crest of Waterloo the English square held with the same tenacity, its wounded and dead drawn quietly in as the human walls contracted: and the men who stood so firmly were not carefully chosen: they were – Wellington said, who loved them – 'the scum of the earth'. What made them fight so well?

They were led by the most mysterious of earthly powers – the influence of one human being over another; and in these ultimate examples, when the net is one of life and death and death is willingly chosen, the power must surely be drawn from some strangely unassailable stronghold. Into it, as into a reservoir undisclosed but ever available, the Leader dips and emerges, unconscious of his divinity as the shipwrecked Ulysses when the goddess threw majesty upon him. For it is not the conscious effort that gives the quality of leadership; no political or artistic trick, no conforming with public opinion or taste will secure it: but where it exists it creates a pull, an approach, a yearning however ignorant of the smallest streamlet thirsting for its sea. The thirst is awakened and the miracle happens, as exciting as the miracle of growth – reality stirring reality.

The foreign quality of this elusive gift is shown, I think, by its aloofness – an independence of anything we might call ethical which it shares with the greatest earthly powers, with the justice that is not our justice, with the shining of the sun on right and wrong, with life itself that floods upon us pressing irresistible through the world's concrete walls. Active yet remote, like all these hidden but familiar forces, the foreign gift of leadership can inspire the saint or help the sinner with equal efficiency and rouse an equally selfless loyalty for either. The leader, whatever he is, as he steps out on to his stage, holds the knife of the Borgias in his hand, of which one side was safe and the other poison; which of them he has chosen is hidden in his heart and, as often as not, from himself.

We can see therefore that leadership is not a virtue on its own account, but an *instrument*, a weapon or a tool, powerful for good or evil as any nuclear discovery, and so potent that one can imagine even the Olympians feeling something like dismay at its appearance. Some defence must be found, one imagines they agree, as they lean from their high places and watch the inspired armies, men and ideas or weapons or arts contending, till earth itself threatens to be torn apart. The palliative they found was a freedom, the freedom of choice.

This was that deliberate choice which Beatrice, the democratic, aristocratic Florentine, held to be the 'noble virtue', and humanity in its dim way has accepted it as a prerogative worth dying for. Dante describes it – 'that innate freedom' – at the end of Purgatory when Vergil takes his leave:

Leadership

Onde, poniam che di necessitate
Surga ogni amor che dentro a voi s'accende,
Di ritenerlo è in voi la podestate.

(Grant then, that from necessity arise
All love that glows within you; to dismiss
Or harbour it, the power is in yourselves).
Purgatorio. xviii, 68–72.
H. F. Cary trans.

It is surprising how lightly this gift is taken. The Leader is drawn by his capacity and the bias that is in him, and it is often too late when he notices how their choice was not intrinsically his own; but because of his gift the virtue or the wickedness of others will tread in his footsteps, and there can be fewer regrets more bitter than those of a true Leader who has used his ambiguous weapon unconsciously on the poisoned side. The nemesis lies between him and his gods, and the burden is his to carry: but the 'followers' are not called upon to discover the origin of their devotion at its source: they need no theology to keep along the pathway of their saint, no strategy to fight in their captain's ranks; they are looking (they feel, if they are true followers) from their own shadow into light, stepping into a radiant irresponsibility which sometimes leads to paradise and quite often leaves an annihilated world behind it: good or bad, the soul of the follower in its unquestioning loyalty is safe.

Happy are they who can look back with quiet hearts to the beginning of this journey and feel the magic of their Leader's presence as they felt it at the first. But there are many, who gradually see that the roads they tread are turning to wildness around them, the water-holes lost or dry, and in the thirst and agony of a desert end they recognize the city of their longing to be a rootless and insubstantial mirage in their sky. It is this supreme tragedy which the freedom of Choice is furnished to avoid. The Leader is far ahead, and all life's possibilities and dangers tossing round him, yet the choice must be made: ragged and poor as we may be, we must stand beside him, for a flash, an instant – merely to see whether his road and ours are still the same.

8

The Written Word

It is better for thee to cast a stone at random than a word.

PORPHYRY to Marcella, 14.

Or do you imagine that it makes no difference with what words you bring about what can only be brought about by words?

FRONTO to M. Aurelius, II, 59.

A s one looks across the ruined landscapes of Central Asia, and even more so at windswept spaces where the rich cities stood, one would think that Time should be the Presence mostly in our sight. But it is not so. Not what *is*, but what has been left out remains with us – an emptiness built by footsteps that have trodden there, a yapping of caravans as in Stravinsky's music, the steppes and their endless transition where Time never stays long enough to matter: we see his coming and his going, but what remains in our heart is the solitude, where the barking of dogs lasted longer than the massacre of men,* and nomad flocks now pasture in the gates of Balkh or Samarkand. It is the *absence* of Time that we notice.

Ever on the edge of a frontier, Diyarbekr, the Roman Amida, was a city, says Ammianus† 'remembered for its misfortune' in the Persian siege from which he himself escaped. It stands on low headlands where the Tigris

---

* See the *Travels of an Alchemist*, trans. Arthur Waley, from the Chinese, p. 111.

† Ammianus Marcellinus, XVIII, 8, 16.

breaks from hills, with deserts of Syria in the south: and later centuries of war have pushed up to it a thin quick population still speaking its Arab language, but now mixed with Turkish beneath the magnificent Seljuk inscriptions that crown the Byzantine walls.

I was wandering here one morning, looking up at their splendour and stepping carefully, since the Eastern insouciance had decreed this to be the rubbish area of the town; and there among the mounds of refuse I saw a thin young man, evidently poor, who had picked up the scrap of some magazine and was reading it with passionate attention.

I passed by him unnoticed. His absorption touched me, I think of it now, when I am saddened by what we do to our printed words. For that capacity for enthusiasm and absorption is a human capacity, especially in the young, and is treated far worse than were the walls of Diyarbekr with their printed rubbish. I have long come to believe that, more than any other destruction, our word-reckless-ness is endangering the future of us all.

Thought, abstract thought (even my dog does quite a lot of *concrete* thinking), was imagined by Aristotle to be the only key to immortality: he suggested it non-committingly, for he was not what you might call a believer. The human mind alone can help us to overstep the edge of infinity; and by using it, says Aristotle, 'we obtain as much im-mortality as we can'. When we do so, unburdened by Space or Time, we shall presumably be able to commu-nicate without instruments, and truth or falsehood will be automatically clear – a bracing prospect, no doubt, to the courageous: but meanwhile, in this hampered world, *no tools other than written or spoken words exist for the expression of thought*; and I would ask any candid reader to look round and see what we have done with them.

I used to ponder this question while going around in

London undergrounds and watching people as they restored themselves with the evening press at the end of the day. In the idleness of transportation I studied the reverse side of their papers and found comfort in the good stolidity of faces whose reading capacities had obviously not been much penetrated: they would have been thinking more coherently if they were lacing up their shoes, I reflected: and yet they were sensible people – family fathers, women with bags and baskets, youth setting out on its life road – their capacities all enveloped in the Evening Mercury or whatever it might be. If this civilization strengthens all over the world, I remember thinking, the human race will fade off its surface like the dinosaurs, and Timelessness will have to find some other forms in which to discover its own immortality all over again.

It was in these moments that the image of the thin young reader among the refuse heaps consoled me.

Melancholy however is not to be confined to the reading of evening papers. Their mischief is not, for instance, universal like that of advertisement which has brought our disregard for truth into the open without even a figleaf to cover it. Nor is it as bad as nearly all the literature you buy at any Italian railway station. Nor really as bad as many things that clever people write. But it is designed to reach the taste and keep to the level of the average man, whose status, 'all comeliness and grace in the image of God' has deteriorated in the eyes of editors since Milton wrote.

This loss of status is emphasized by the fact that the written word is no longer intended to do anyone any particular good. It is useful for practical and scientific proficiency, but its great empire has gone down like our own, and whole realms – such as history – are no longer those white spaces where lessons might be discovered for future as well as past. Philosophy is linguistics as in many a declining age before it, helpful neither in daily life nor death; and when the theologians get together the tone of even the Bible's organ voice is lowered:

'Through the tender mercy of our God,
Whereby the dayspring from on high hath visited us,
To give light to them that sit in darkness and in the shadow of death'

The new English version says:

'For in the tender compassion of our God the morning sun from heaven will rise upon us, to shine on those who live in darkness under the cloud of death.' (Luke I, 78–9)

The meaning is almost the same only dimmed; the passion is snuffed; the beauty lessened; we must take our bread without butter and be thankful that the bread remains.

A number of other instances might be added to this gloomy collection if one tended to lament; and one may say, though I do not like to do so, that timeless truth is not nor ever can be found till Time is overstepped.

But it has often been sought for. And it is not widely sought for now. Scientific truth is sought for; but that belongs to Time and Space, and is as much of a 'documentary' as are the hands of a clock in relation to the machinery that makes them tell the hours. I am digging deeper for the root of the paralysis that has smitten our words, our only vehicles of thought, nursed from animal to man and set to deposit us safely on that bank where Space and Time must stop. At the cross-roads where Hercules' choice was made and every creature's choice before and after, some wrong turning surely was taken? The words slipped from the care that had held them through the unlettered ages, that had reached the Mediterranean headlands, the Indian riverlands, the shores of Galilee, the

Mecca sand – all the peoples of their books in all their habitations. Having done their work there, and seen Europe through its childhood and America started, the words are stumbling on now under a new guide.

Writers have not voluntarily betrayed them. The author's profession is not so generally profitable as to make an element in his preference, and even a poor author has his visions. But the machine is now nearly out of his hands and his choice at the cross-roads is very hard indeed. To risk security and comfort when one is not even sure that the result may not be mediocrity or worse, is every artist's obstacle at his beginning, and the real choice, the temptation to compromise, comes only later, when he has learnt what he would say (or paint or carve or sing) if his road were clear. It is then, if ever, that the Tempter can get him.

The Tempter is not conscious as a rule of the murder he is committing. He is anxious first and foremost to make money, but he would also like to encourage Art and the author, and he has his organizations that are there for the artist and his public to meet. The devil, I believe, is not as wicked as he is painted and is apt to be amiable at heart. That the excellent cannot also be average is a fact that he regrets (in a vague way, for he is not always sure of the excellent when he sees it): but he would help it if he could, if the law of *supply and demand* would allow it.

Now this is the crux of the problem, for the law of supply and demand is indeed a good law and one which the peoples and their books have followed through the ages when the great books were written – (no demand for instance could have been greater than that for the Ten Commandments supplied to a public unconscious of its need). When we look into this problem we notice that it is a matter of precedence, and the law is correctly stated: the supply artist with his work comes first, and his work must be good enough for the demand to follow. The false step was taken when this order was reversed and the modern world began to use its organizing power to create an unfounded and unskilled demand: the elder brother, Supply, now follows as best he can while the young Caracalla* (who murdered his elder brother) takes his place. By this single transposition, Supply and the artist are reduced from free agent to slaves.

The murder was inflicted not on them but on their words. Style cannot be organized; no wealth of efficiency seems able to confer that halo of its glory on an epoch – not Napoleon with all Europe at his feet. The feather words are blown by a far wind. They travel from ages before they were invented and stretch in their causes from the beginning of Time to its end. Not the most vulgar advertiser from America or Europe would paste up his slogans if he could feel for one instant the majesty and scope of that progression. Civilization begins to understand that thought is not to be suppressed when truly spoken, and Russia too may win that battle soon. But in the West we have not yet noticed how the easiest way to kill good words is simply to encourage the bad ones, and ours is the more dangerous because the more permanent mistake of the two.

The wastes of Asia are haunted by traces of words the conquerors destroyed. But ours, in Europe left with us in the twin streams of the living and the dead, are still vital in their capacities, still ready for the sculptor's hand. They are more important than all the money the middleman can conjure, and no pathetic government effort is sufficient – only the middleman himself in his own understanding can inspire the massacre to cease.

He is the Tempter, but not wicked, and often though perhaps tepidly on the side of the angels in his heart: and his road has its wayside comforts to be sought for, though its end is that sad vagueness. If the heaps of printed rubbish which he handles were present to his mind as the poison

* Son of Septimius Severus.

which they are, he would not present them to his fellow men for any reward at all.

In my long life I have been fortunate to miss the Tempter's wiles; poverty has sometimes looked in and thrown its obstacles, but it has never been brutal enough to compel me to stand against myself; as far as I can say it, everything good or bad that I have written has come willingly from my heart. But among the crowds I have met – friends often heroic – many nobler and finer than I am have bowed their heads; and I think of them 'rising from their retreat like a wind'* in the serenity not of their lives but of their longing, and fed not with the words of which fate or weakness or cruelty deprived them, but with the ardour of their dream.

But most often I think of the thin young man so poorly dressed lost in his scrap of rubbish beneath the great Byzantine walls.

* Demosthenes: 'The Crown'.